Aux Arcs

Black & White Photography Of The Ozarks Region

Carl James

Edited by:
Leila Parker & Jana Duke

Foreword by:
David Catlin

Published by:
JEC Publishing Co

JEC PUBLISHING COMPANY
2049 E. Cherry Street
Springfield, Missouri 65802
(800) 313-5121
www.jecpubco.com

Library of Congress Control Number: 2009933651

ISBN: 978-0-9824801-2-0

Concept, Author, Photos and Cover by: Carl H. James and Liteworx Productions

Prepared for Publishing by: JE Cornwell and Tom Dease

Printed in Canada

DEDICATION

This book is dedicated to my
sister LaVonna (James) Mincks who
shared my love for nature

WHAT IS LIFE?

It is the flash of a firefly in the night.
It is the breath of a buffalo in the wintertime.
It is the little shadow that runs across
the grass and loses itself in the sunset.
Crowfoot, Blackfoot Warrior 1830-1890

FOREWORD

I first got to know Carl James—was it 15 years ago? 20?—when a friend invited us both along on an Arkansas backpacking trip. We discovered we had a mutual love of the Ozarks landscape, and a shared enjoyment of exploring it on foot.

Hiking in the Ozarks is usually a spring or fall activity. In spring and fall, the temperatures are pleasantly cool and the ticks and chiggers mercifully mild-mannered. Spring and fall are also the seasons when the Ozark hills are at their most broadly colorful. October and early November gave us burnt orange and gold panoramas that were repeated in April by the subtler hues of the spring leafing-out.

Carl always had his camera along, but—as this book makes clear—he wasn't always thinking about the colors. Carl is an architect by training, and he sees like an architect. He notices the forms, the weighted contrasts of light and dark, the interplay of lines, and—most especially—the details. We see the old Dawt Mill along the North Fork, he catches the tree reflected in its upstairs window.

I recall one hike in particular where, apparently, he and I were both focused on the details. Carl was always that way; my excuse, I think, was that it was morel mushroom season and I was on the alert for some tasty supplements to our freeze-dried backpacking dinner. Whatever the distractions were, he and I fell behind the rest of our hiking buddies, and then absent-mindedly took a right fork in the trail where they had all taken the left.

FOREWORD continued

Carl and I wandered miles in the wrong direction before it dawned on us that something wasn't right, and we turned around to retrace our steps. Finally straggling into camp as darkness began to fall, we had to endure an evening of aching feet and the good-natured ridicule of our comrades.

There were compensations, though: I had morels, and Carl had photos.

I don't know if any of those pictures have found their way into this book, but lots of others have. Carl has captured the character and soul of his native landscape, illuminated through its details. I can tell you, I have gotten lost with Carl in the Ozarks, and it was a good and a memorable experience. Now, here's your opportunity to do the same.

David Catlin
August 2009

INTRODUCTION

Aux Arcs, a name that apparently came from the French exploring the region in the late 1600's and early 1700's. Translated loosely, Aux Arcs was "a place of hills or bows". One interpretation is that the name came from a French pioneer expression "Aux Arkansas", literally meaning "To the Arkansas Mountains". The region was part of what became the Louisiana Purchase, settled by other Europeans, and the name slowly changed to the "Ozarks". Geologically the Ozarks is a broad dome of eroded limestone roughly 47,000 square miles consisting of the St. Francois Mountains, the Salem Plateau, the Springfield Plateau and the Boston Mountains. It covers around one third to one half of Missouri, the upper western region of Arkansas and extends into the northeast corner of Oklahoma. It is a region well watered with clear spring-fed streams with many grist mills, hardwood oak and hickory forests intermixed with yellow pine groves. Due to its karst geology, it has many caves.

My relationship with the Ozarks began 61 years ago in Almartha, Missouri, a tiny hamlet between Ava and Gainesville in Ozark County where my parents lived when I was born. They were both native Ozarkians. I have never left although we moved to Springfield, Missouri, further north in the Ozarks, when I was nine. I grew up with so many first cousins (the offspring of 13 aunts and uncles) that there was always someone to help explore the outdoors. We spent many Sundays at dinner with the grandparents. Both sets lived on farms. I guess I always assumed the outdoor theater I lived and played in would never change.

I married when I was 18, had two great sons, divorced at 25, remarried at 31 and had another great son and have been married 30 years. During this time I pursued a career in architecture, retiring two years ago to realize my other dreams.

INTRODUCTION continued

I began exploring photography when my second wife and I bought a Pentax ME with money we got as a wedding present from my boss. I got serious about photography around 15 years ago when I bought a used Nikon F3 with all the works. I have graduated to a Nikon D70s and a Nikon D300.

My serious photography began as a way to document the many hiking, canoeing, and camping trips we took. Sometime in this process the photography became the primary reason for the trips.

I joined the Southwest Missouri Camera Club, The Springfield Visual Arts Alliance and the Springfield Regional Arts Council where I have had success competing in their juried shows. You will likely see some of my exhibits on the First Friday Art Walk in Springfield.

The Ozarks is a mystical place for me. I try to convey that mysticism in my photographs and poetry. I find that photography has heightened my senses. I now notice the shape of a leaf, the glint and mirrored reflection of water droplets on grass, the sinuous shape of water sculpted rock, and the changing interplay of light and shadow on these and all objects. I am now much more aware of my oneness with all of nature.

My reasons for publishing this book are many, but the primary reason is to heighten the awareness of the viewers by encouraging them to step outside, look and observe the wonders and drama of the natural world and to begin to realize his or her role in the never-ending cycle of nature.

Carl James, A.I.A.

ACKNOWLEDGEMENTS

There are several people who I would like to thank for their encouragement and work on this book. As always, great thanks to my wife, Linda, for encouraging me to make my dreams reality. Linda is always my best critic. Thanks to her sister, Diana, and our friends who have given me a lot of encouragement and flattery. Thanks to Gerry and Rosalie Toler for Gerry's cover design and photography critique and Rosalie's poetry critique. Thanks to my editors Jana Duke, a good friend, and my sister Leila Parker for being willing to appease my fears with the redundancy of two editors. Thanks to David Catlin, naturalist, for his review, encouragement, and foreword. David is truly one with nature, having made it his lifelong commitment. And finally, thanks to all the shop owners, strangers, friends and all who kept saying "You otta do a book!"

≈≈

INFO

If you are interested in purchasing additional books or framed and non-framed matted prints that are in this book, contact the author:

Carl James
1224 W. Burntwood
Springfield, MO 65803
Phone: 417-833-6031

Mobile: 417-839-3016
Website: liteworxproductions.com
Email: carljames@liteworxproductions.com
Blog: blog. liteworxproductions.co

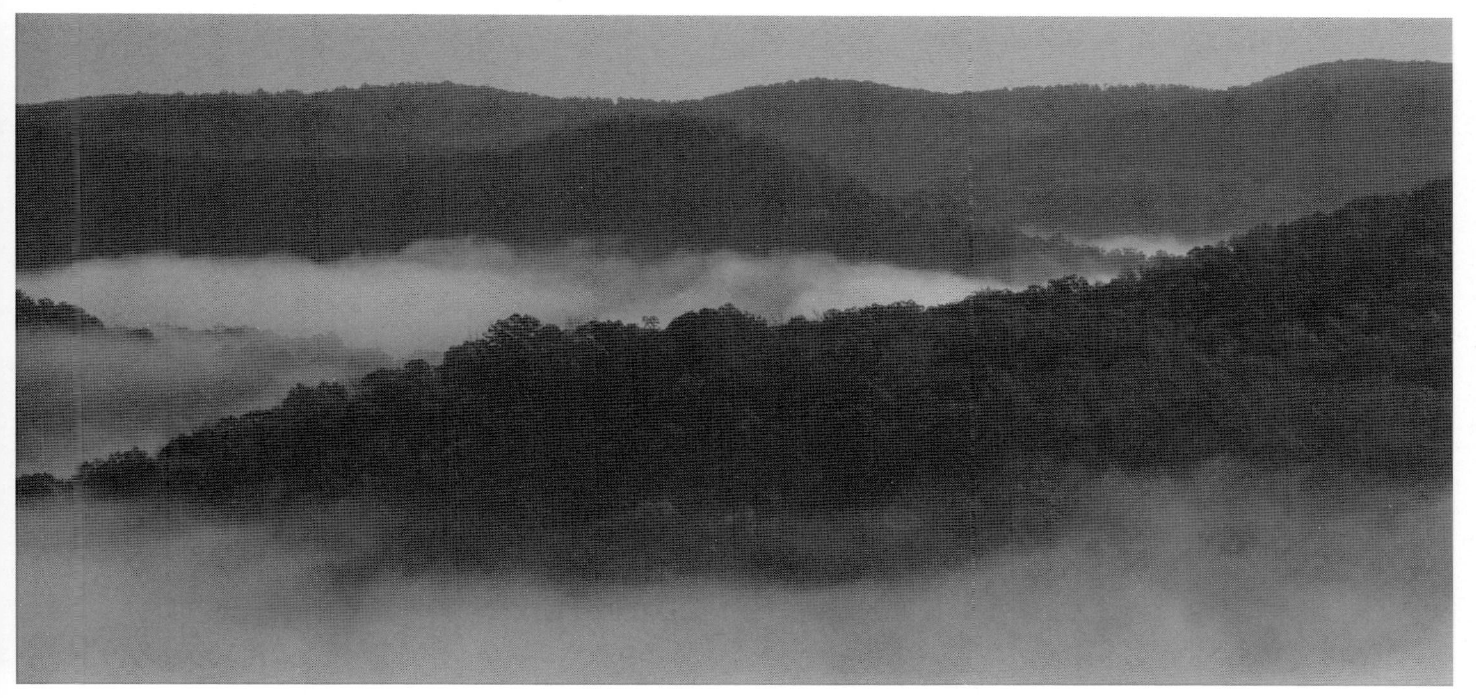

Morning mists viewed from Buffalo Point near Yellville, Arkansas

Morning Mists cloak the valley
like a warm blanket created by the
river protecting its womb of life from
the harsh frosts of the coming winter
Carl James

Magnolia Falls near
Mossville, Arkansas

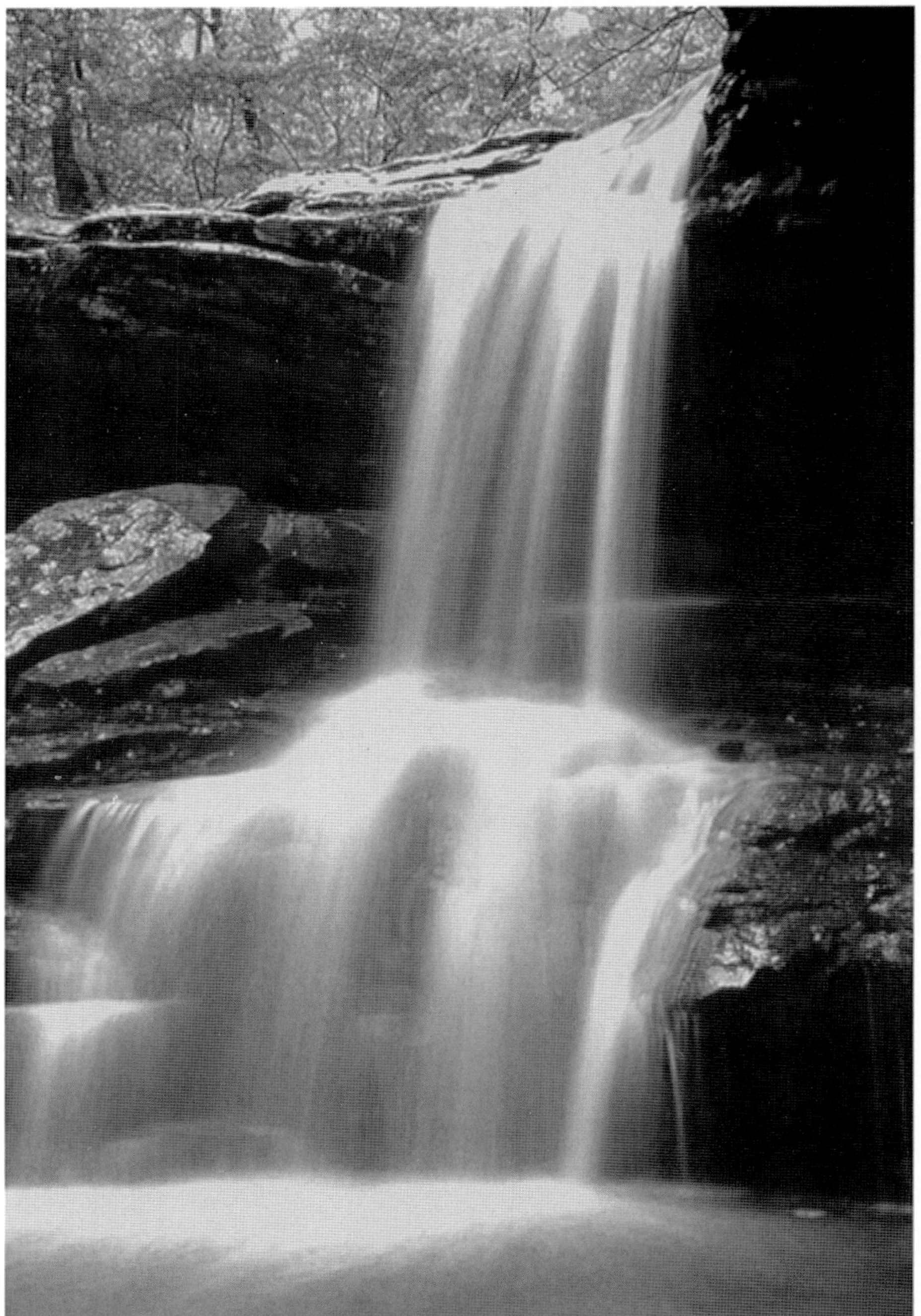

Abandoned house near Reeds Spring, Missouri

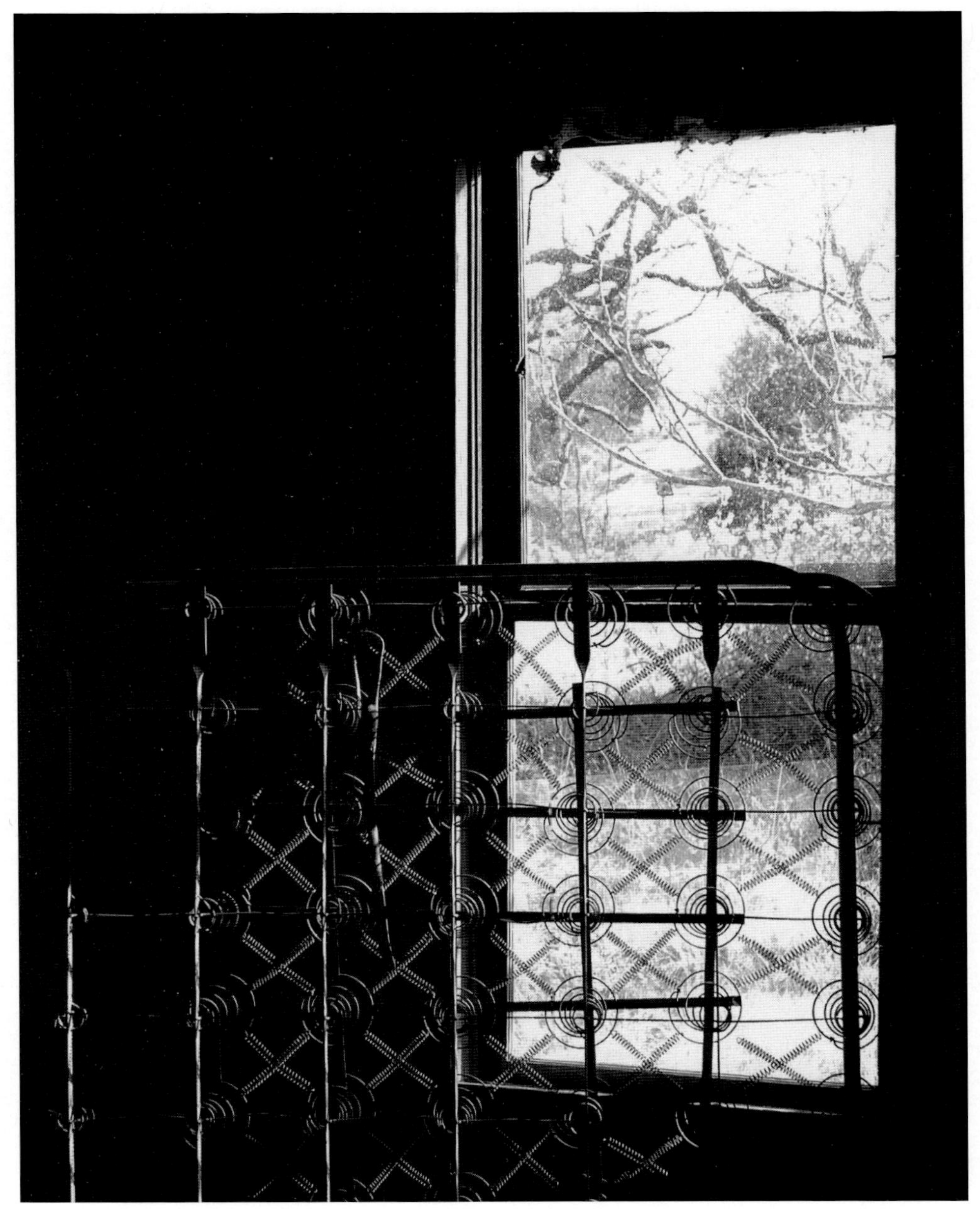

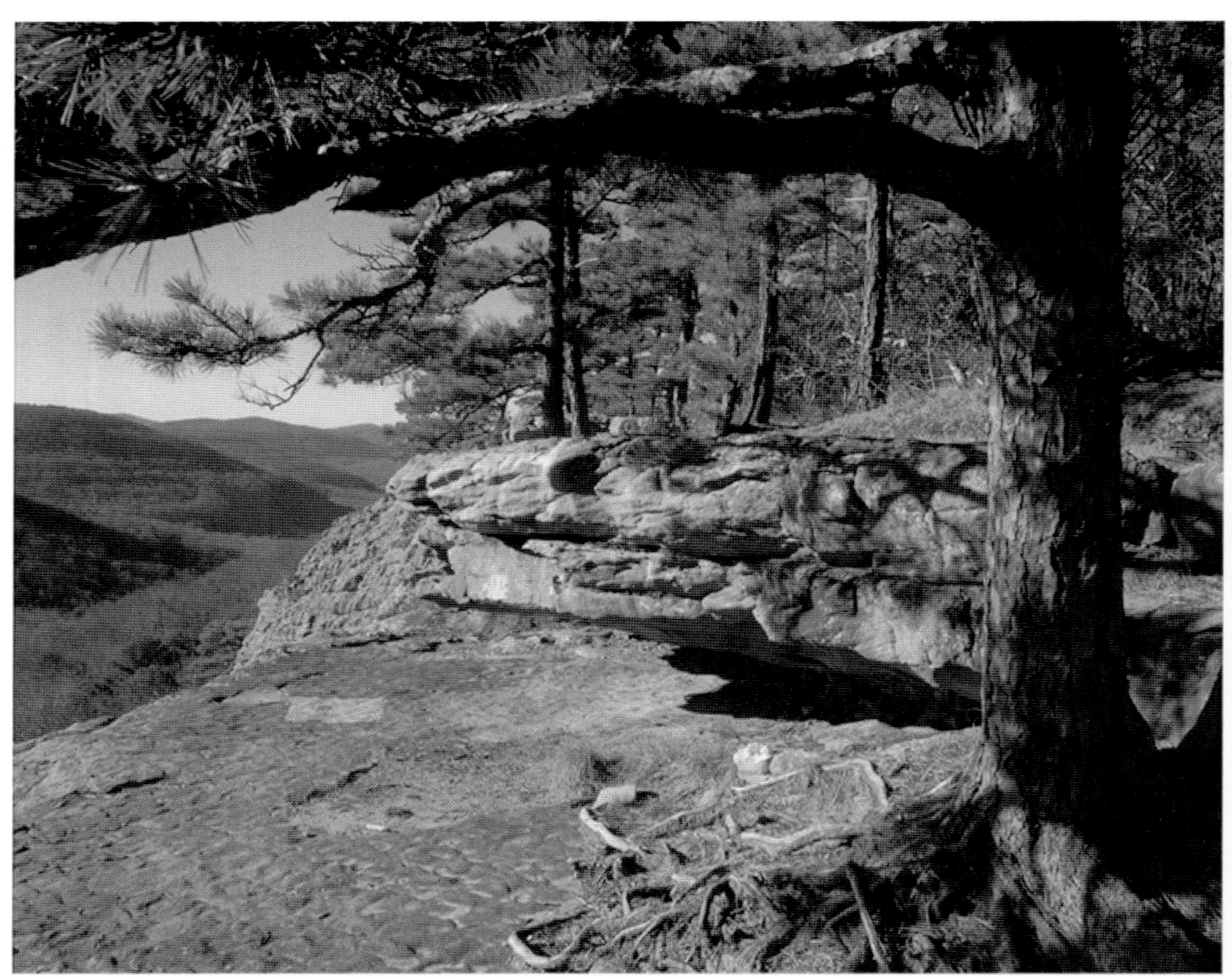

Sam's Throne-Mt. Judea, Arkansas

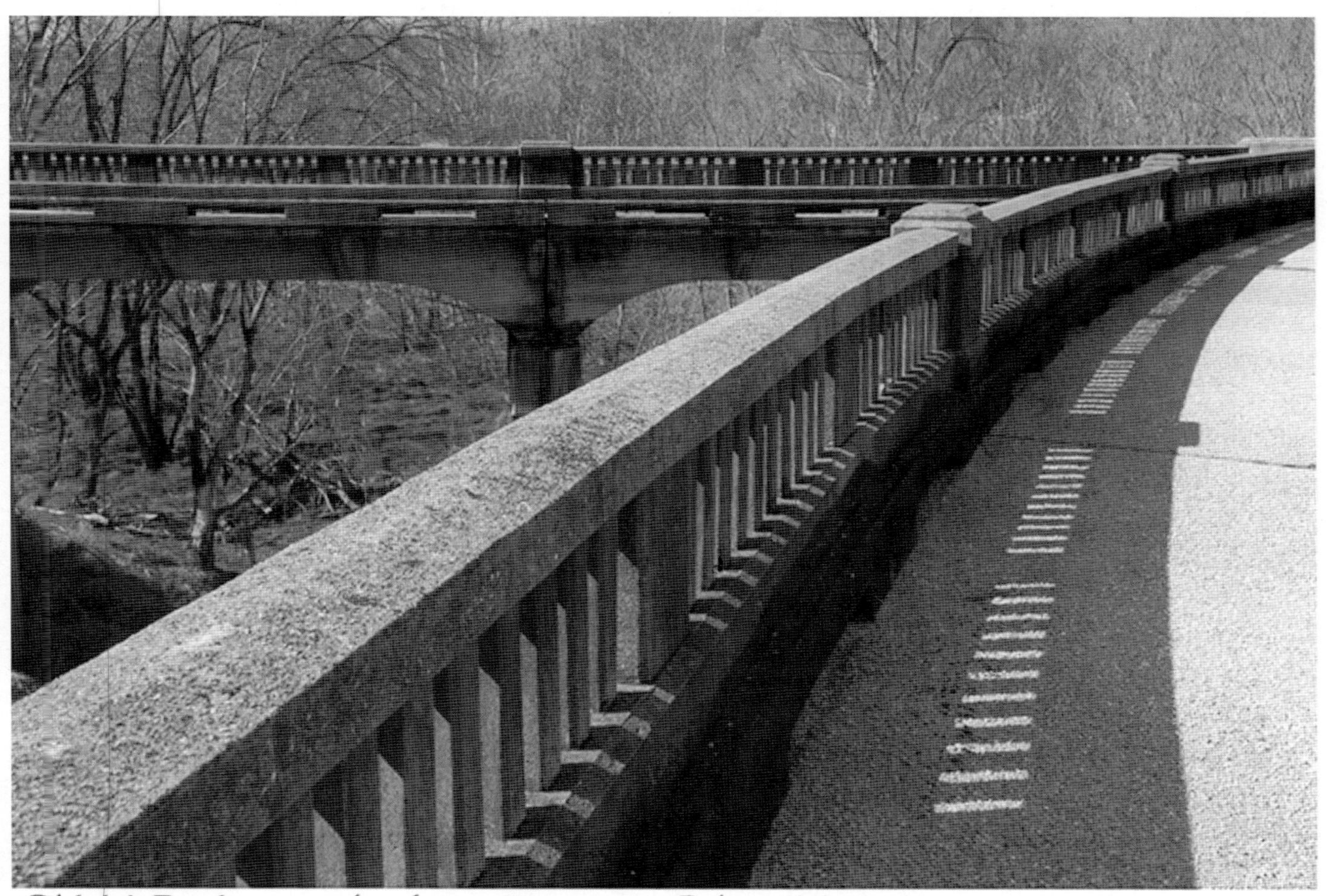

Old "Y" Bridge over the James River near Galena, Missouri

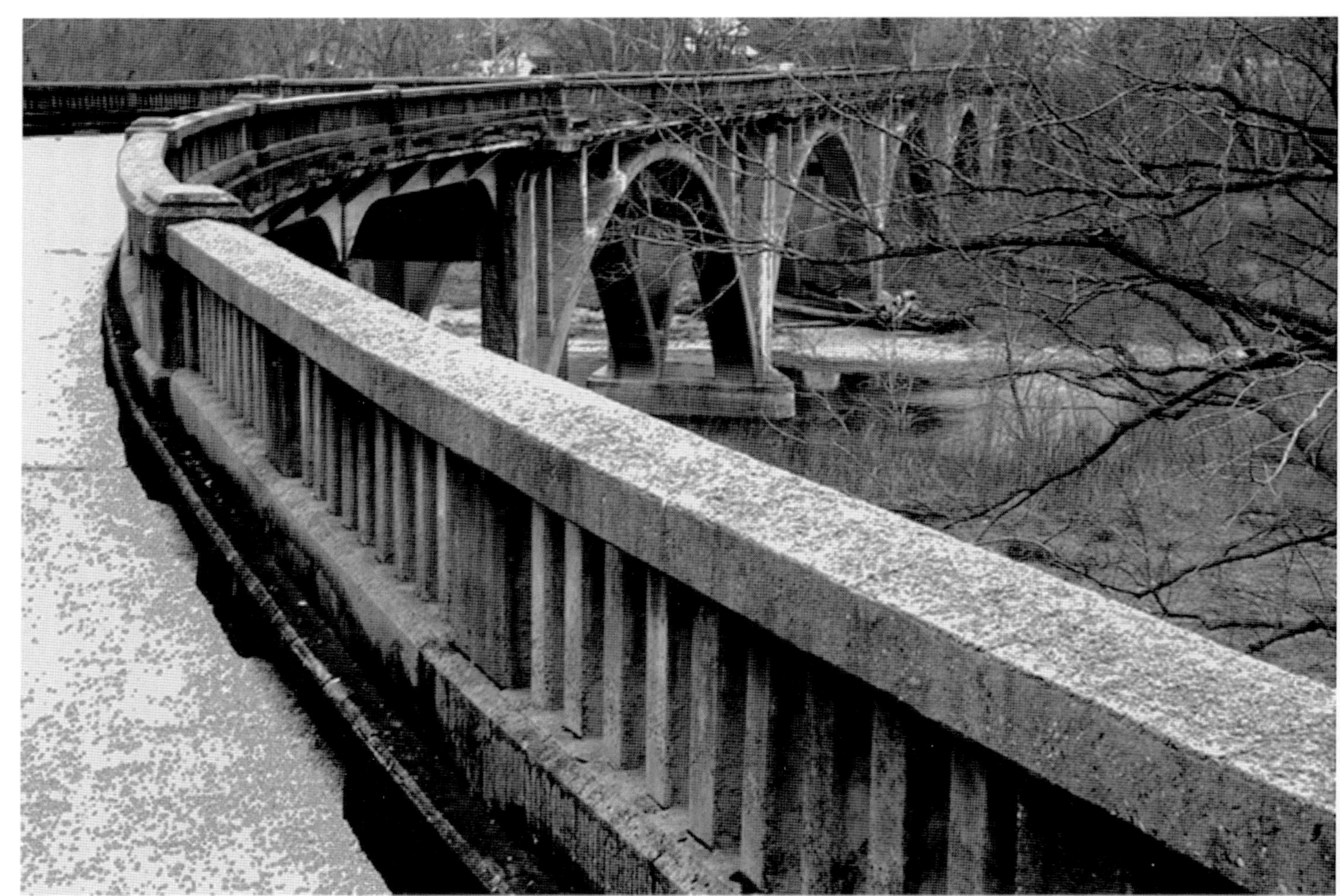

Old "Y" Bridge Crossing the James River in Galena, Missouri

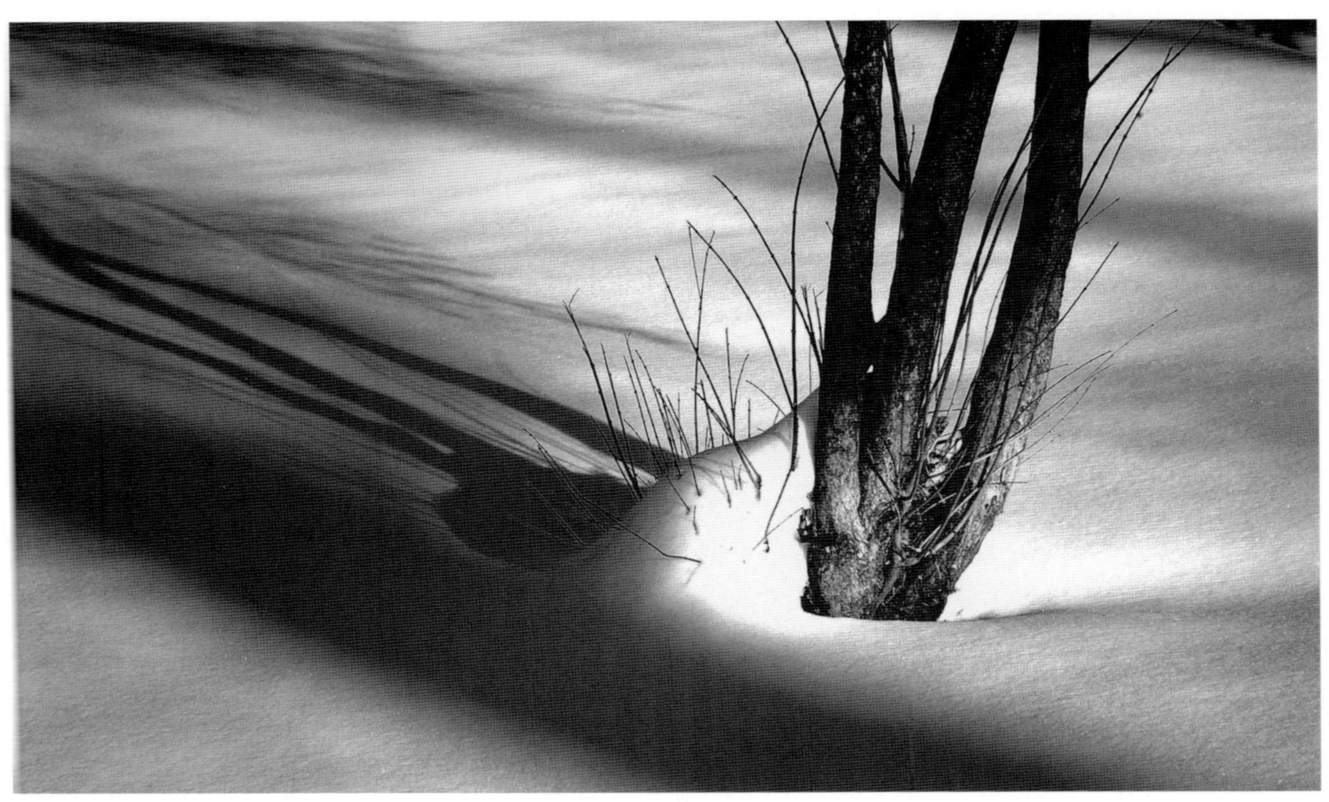

Fassnight Park, Springfield, Missouri

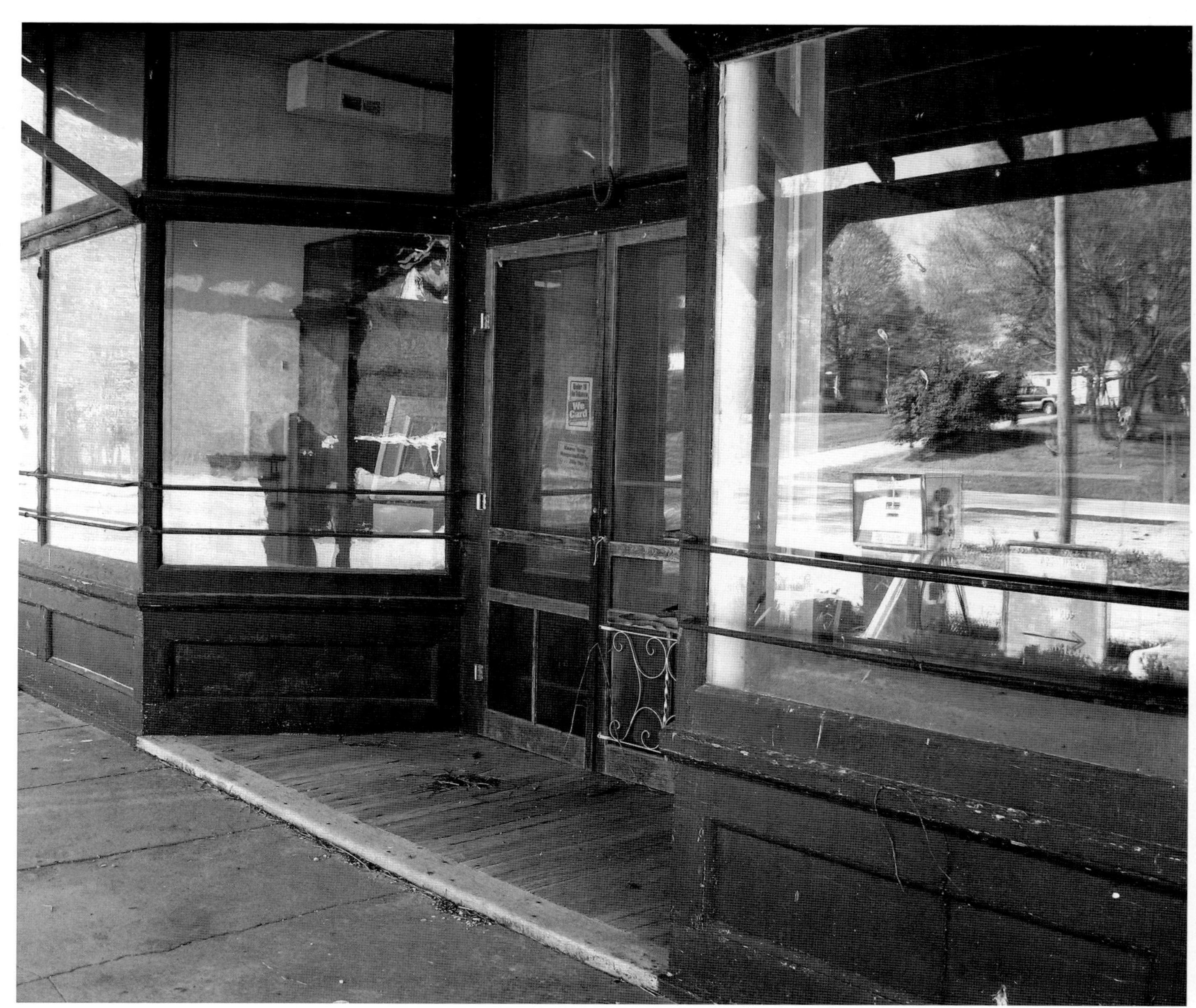

Old General Store-Garrison, Missouri

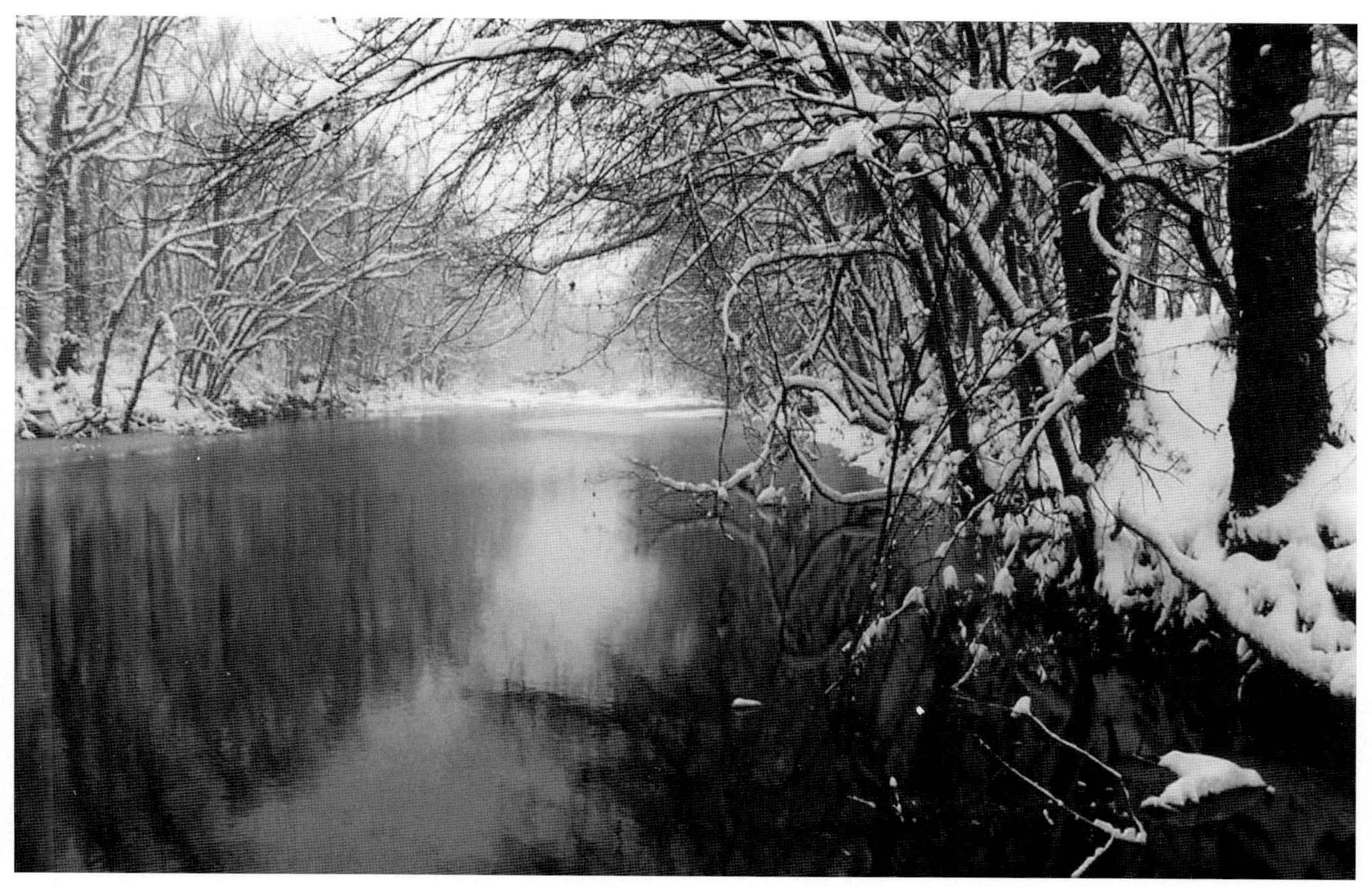

Little Pomme de Terre Creek, near Pleasant Hope, Missouri

Trees bowing in reverence
to the river mirroring
the endless circle of life.
Carl James

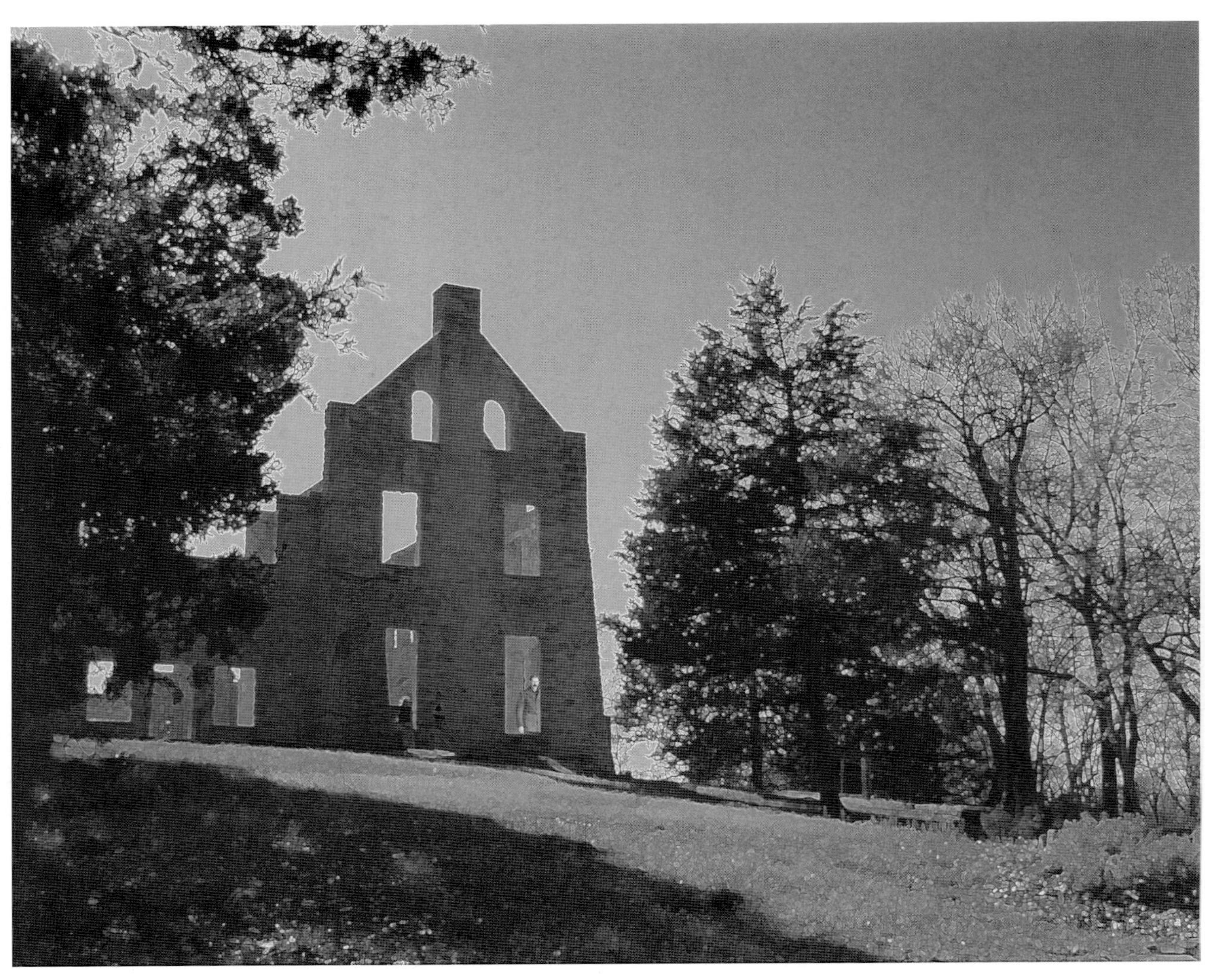

The Sentinel Ha Ha Tonka State Park near Camdenton, Missouri

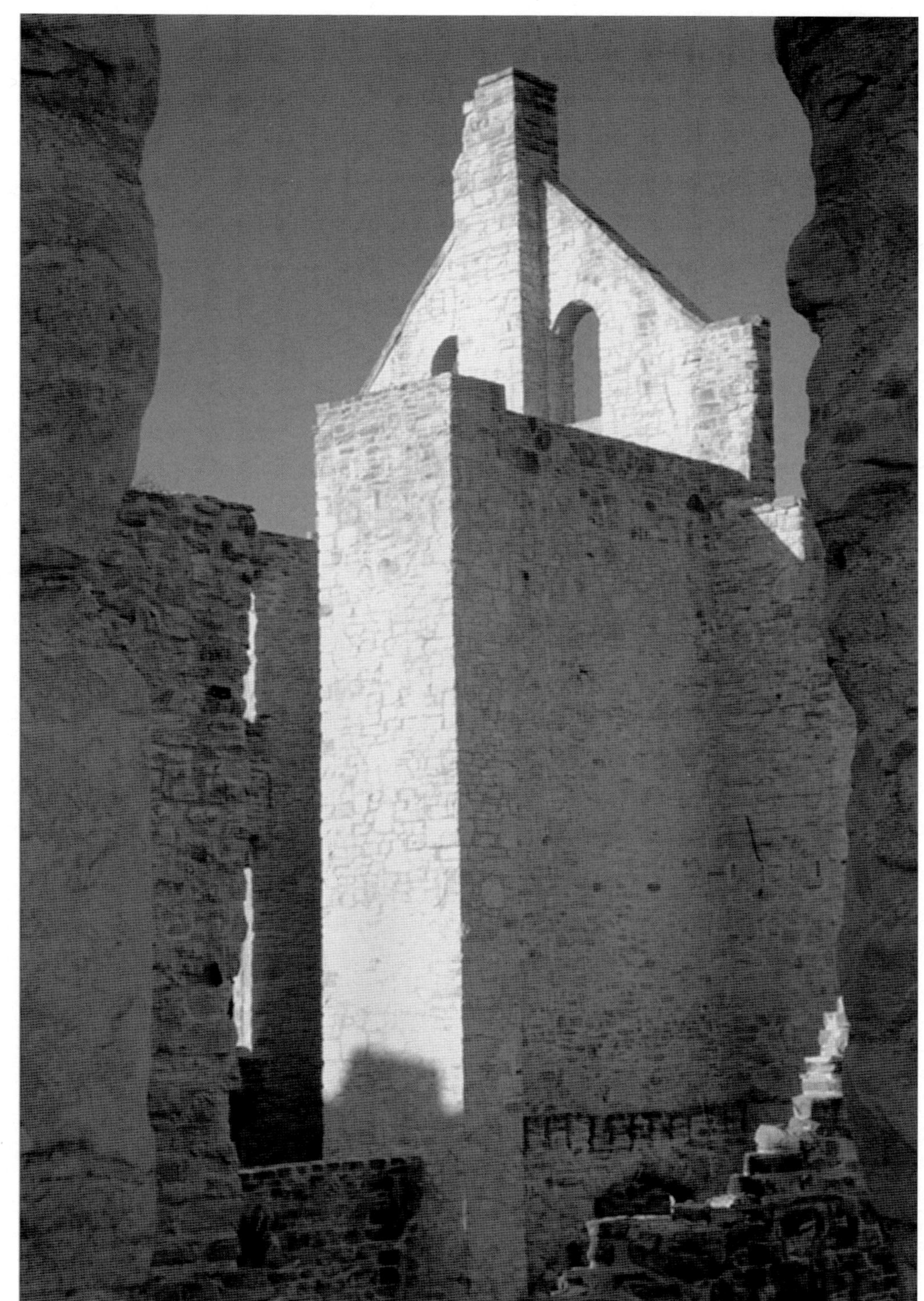

Ha Ha Tonka
Mansion Ruins
Ha Ha Tonka
State Park near
Camdenton, MO

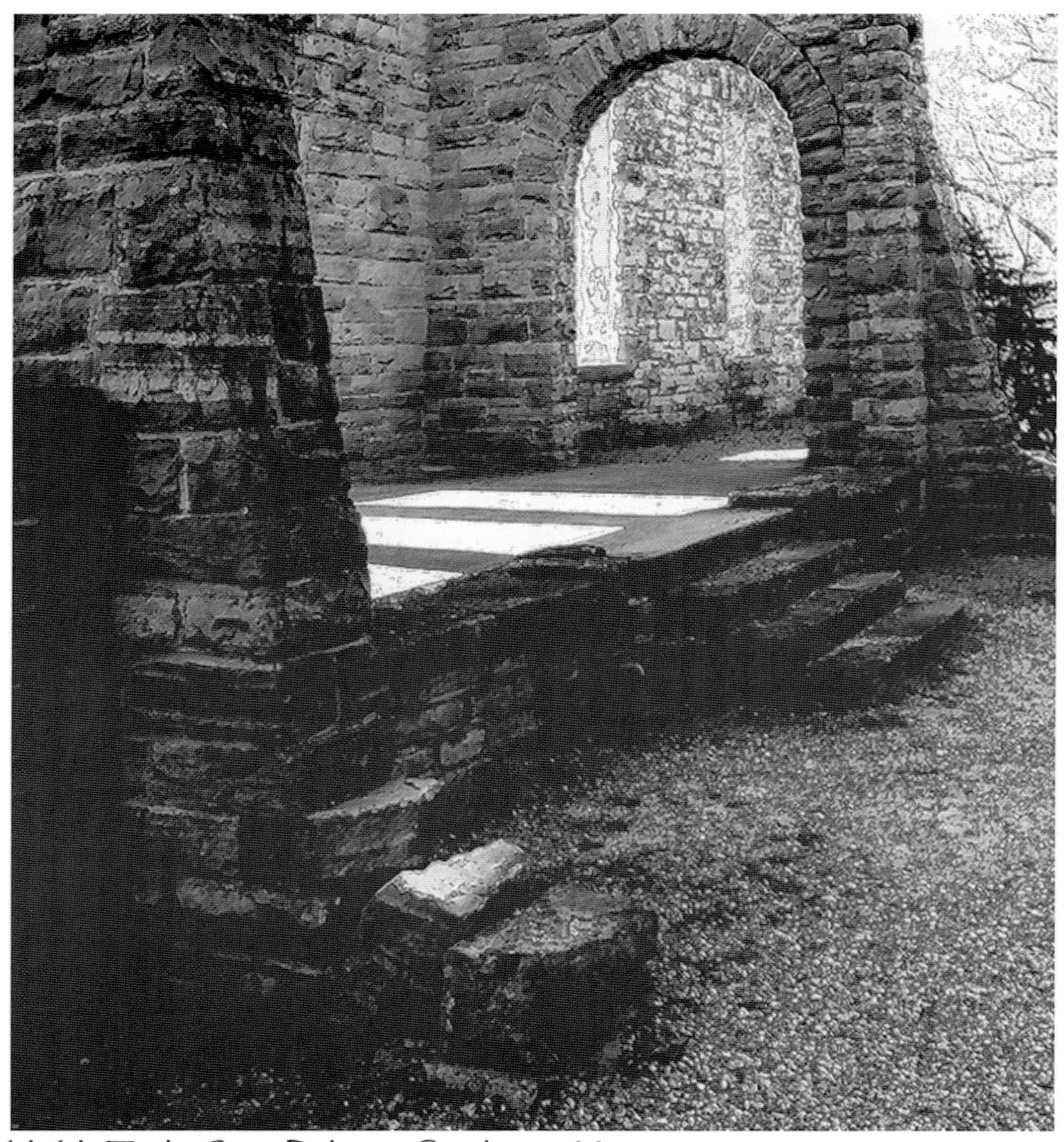

Ha Ha Tonka State Park near Camdenton, Missouri

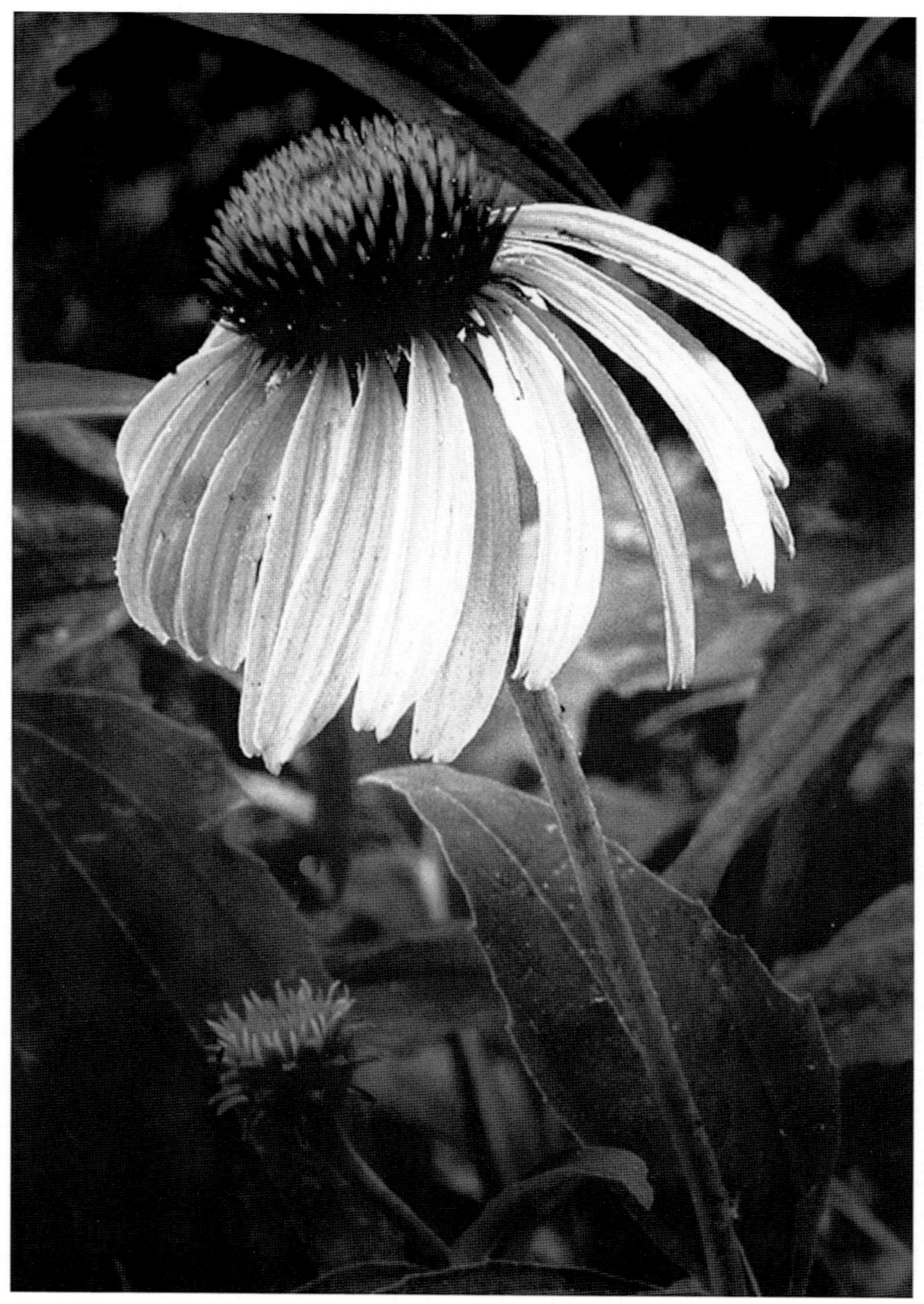

Purple Coneflower

Reaching for the Light

We like trees with one
singular longing

A lifetime of reaching
twisting and bowing

Weathering the storms
Fragile limbs growing

A quest for a life
of loving and knowing

Nourished by the light
Internal and glowing

Replenished by seed
of life's love sowing

Reaching for the stars
An Icarus unknowing

Felled by the light as
Winds for the blowing

Gather your limbs for the
circle of life's flowing

Carl James

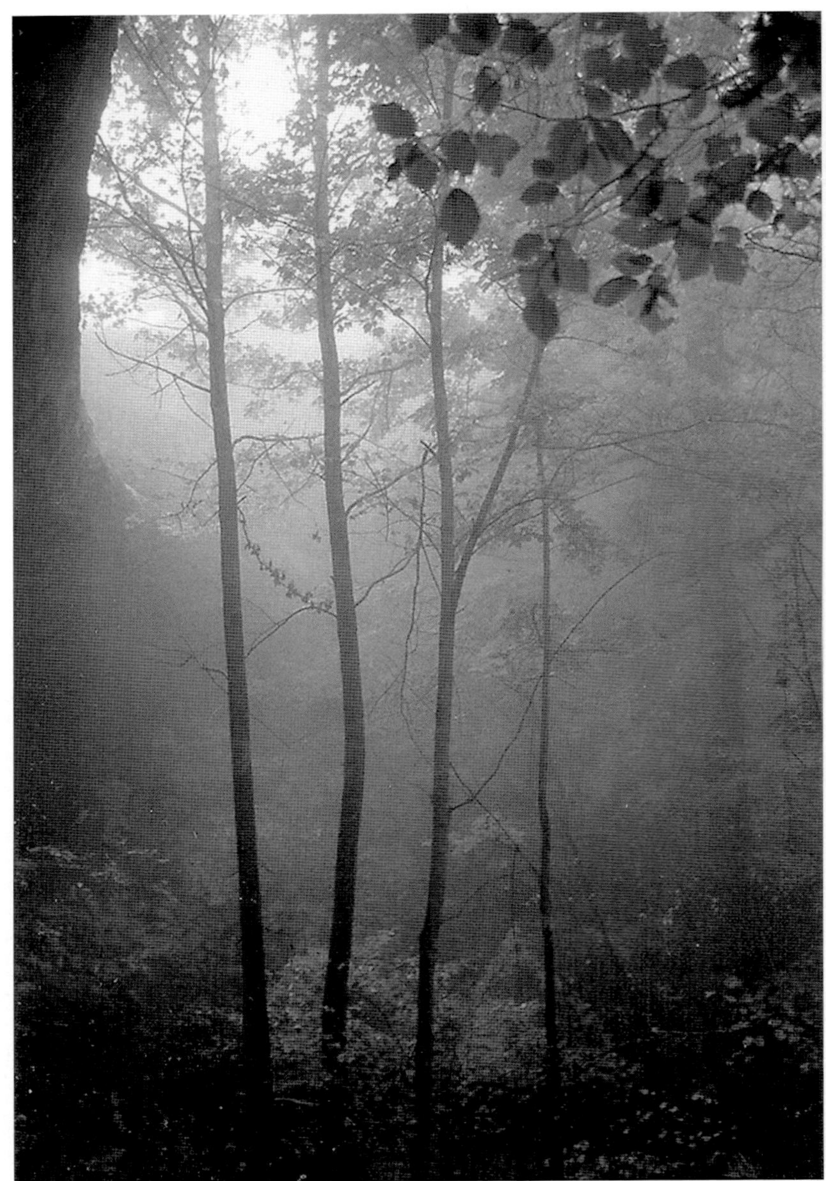

Boen Gulf-Upper Buffalo Wilderness Area

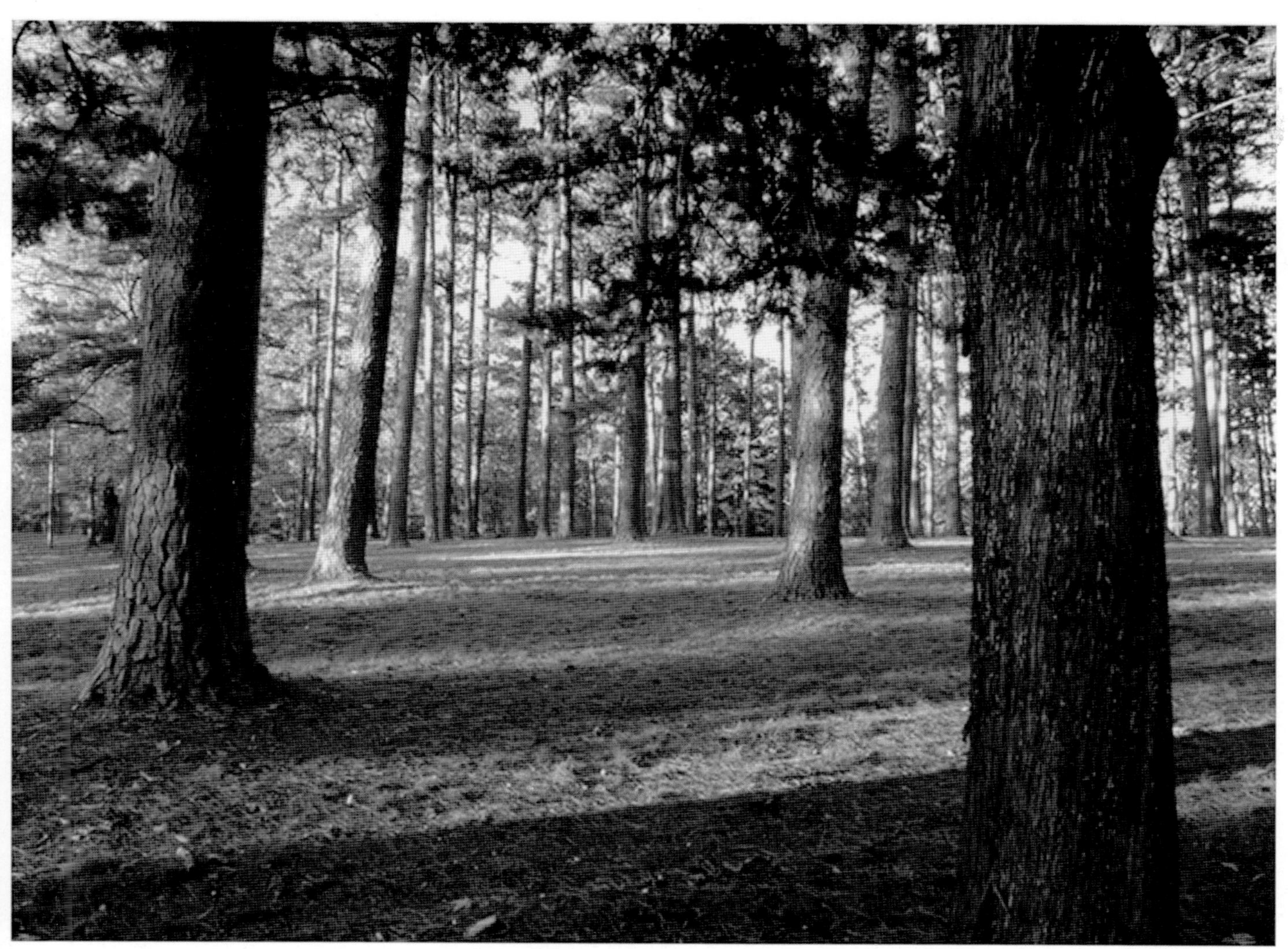

Buffalo Point State Park near Yellville, Arkansas

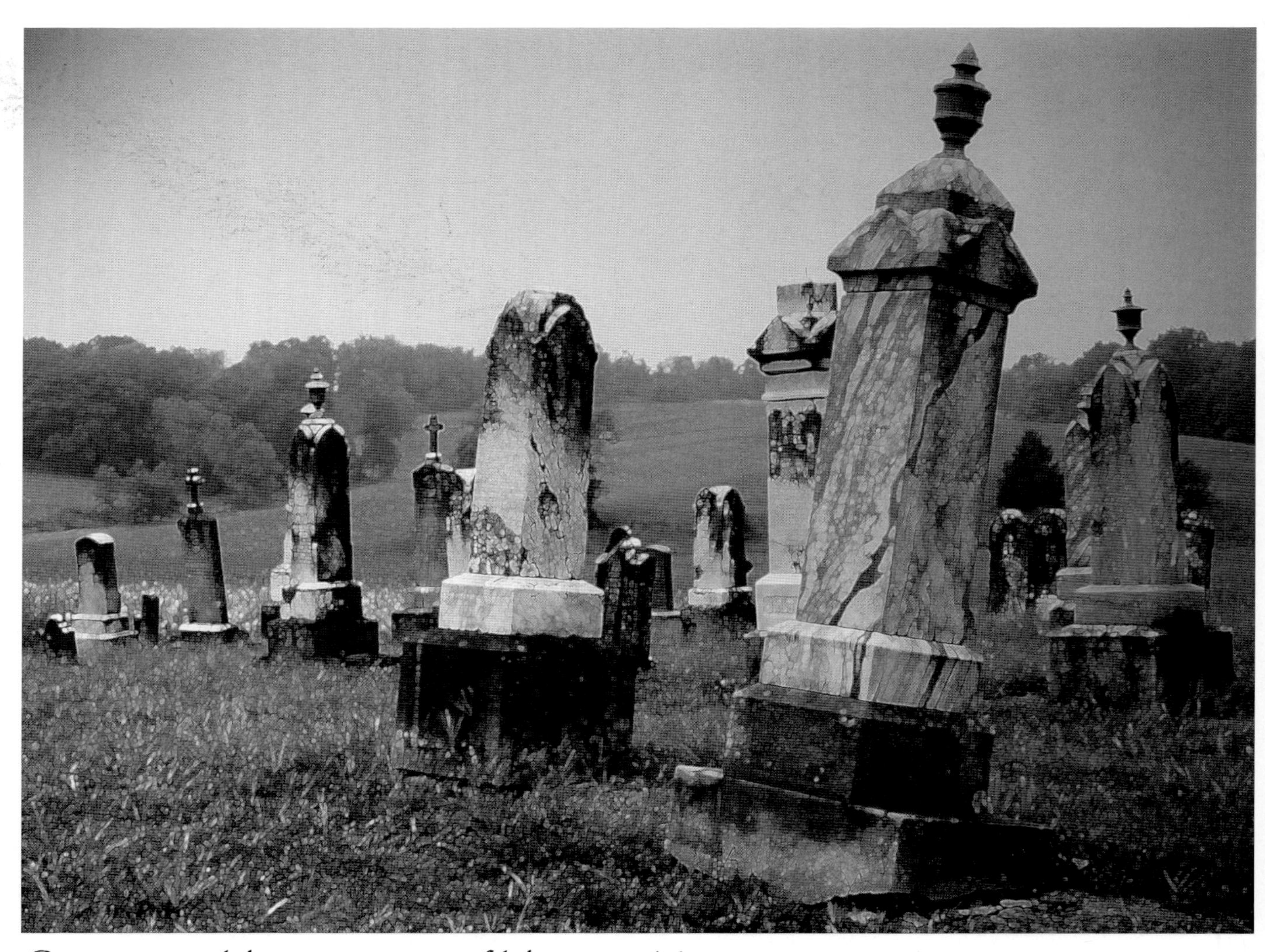

Cemetery on Hwy. #100 east of Hermann, Missouri

A View on the Road to Enlightenment

Fellows Lake near Springfield, Missouri

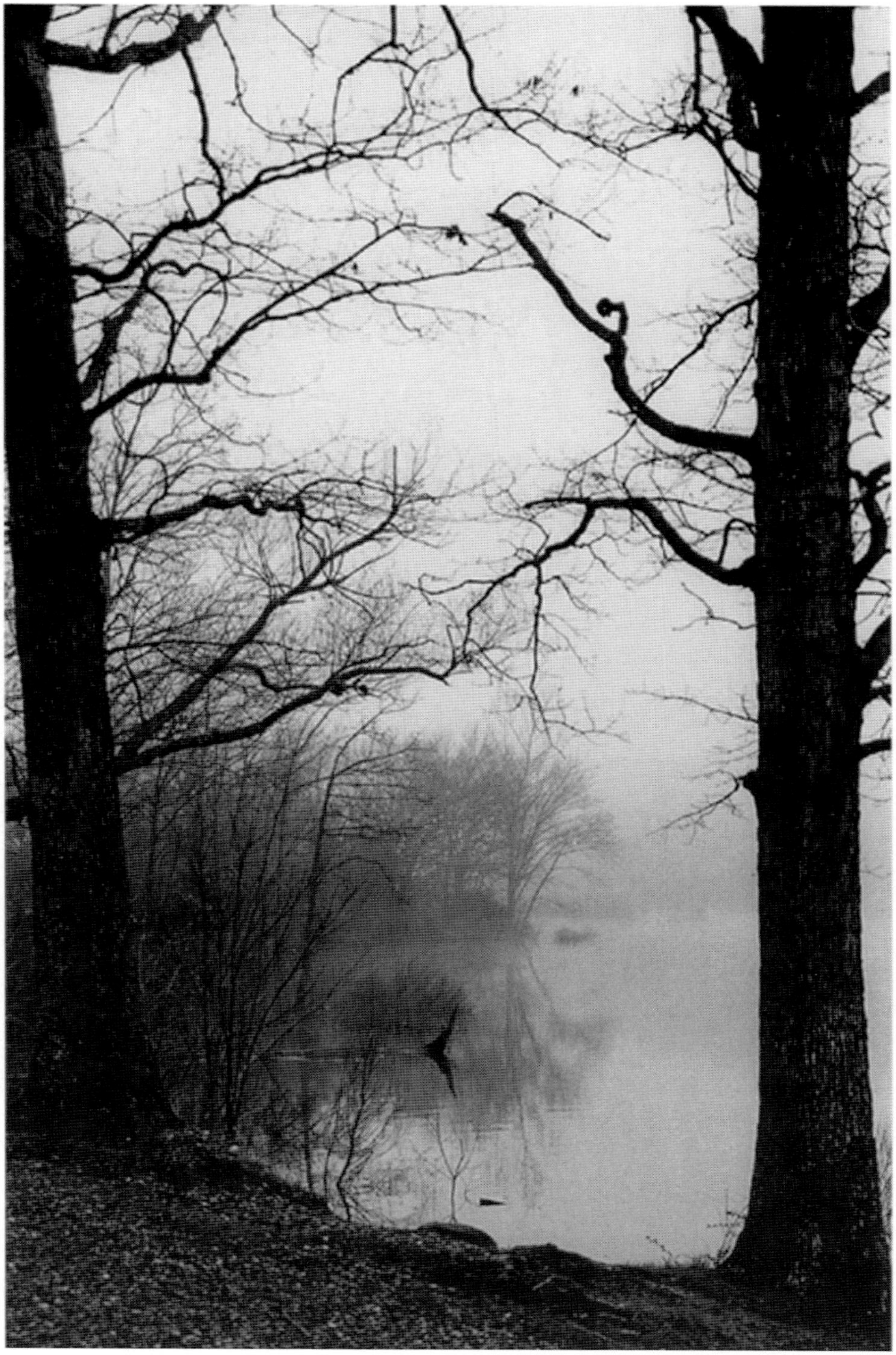

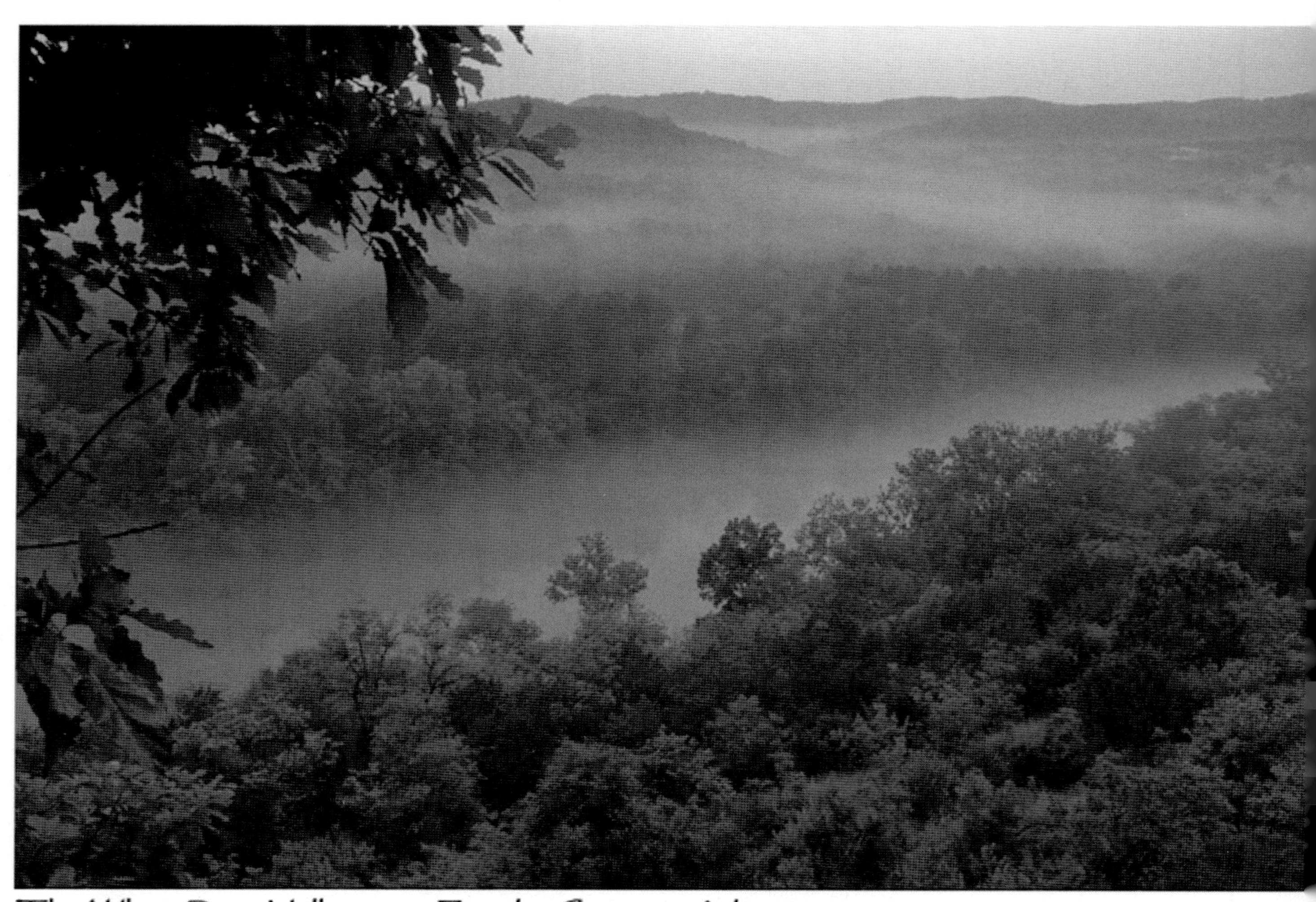
The White River Valley near Eureka Springs, Arkansas

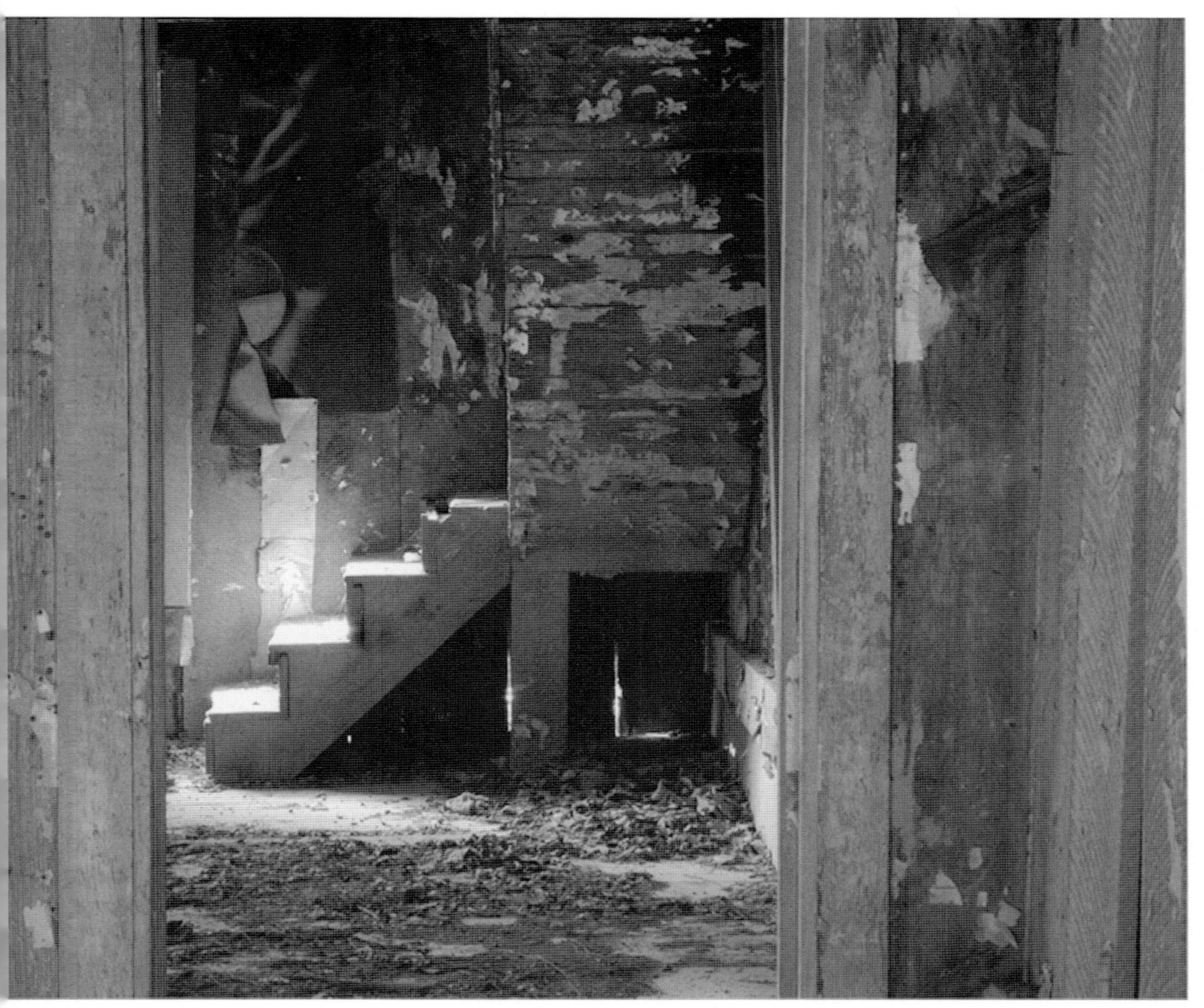

Abandoned Zinc Mining Town-Rush, Arkansas

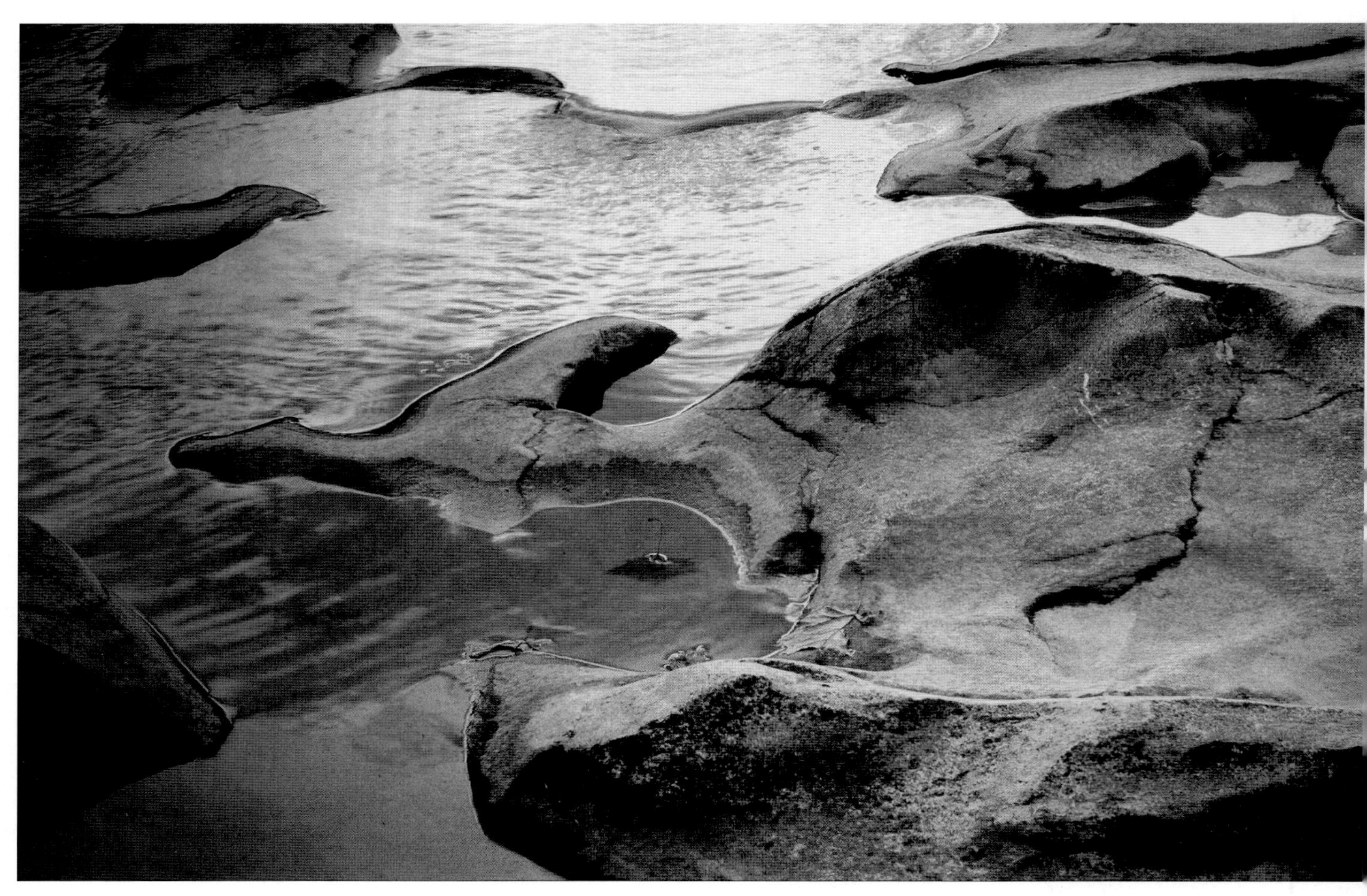

Water Sculpted Rock-Falling Water Creek near Ben Hur, Arkansas

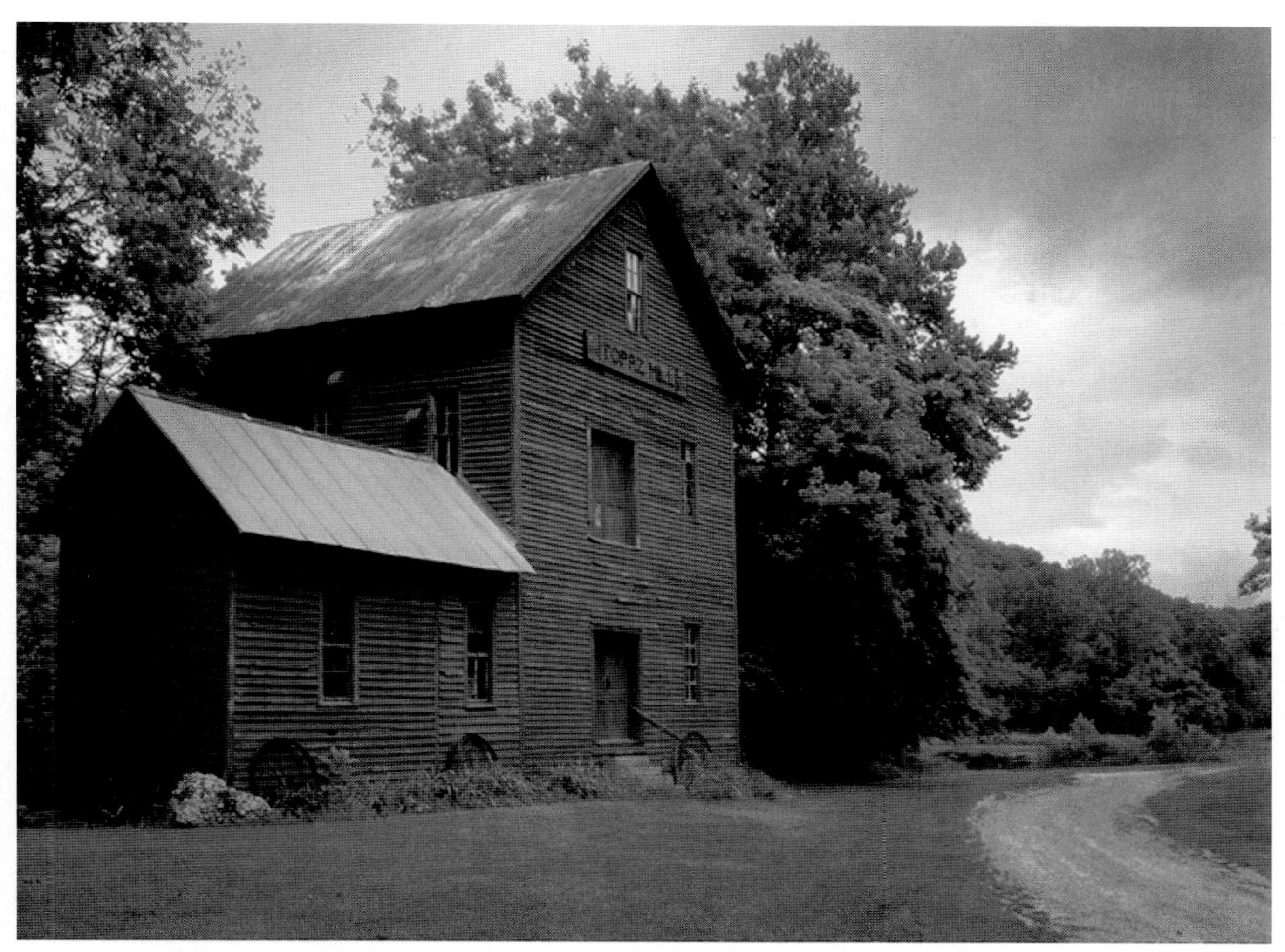

Topaz Mill-Topaz, Missouri

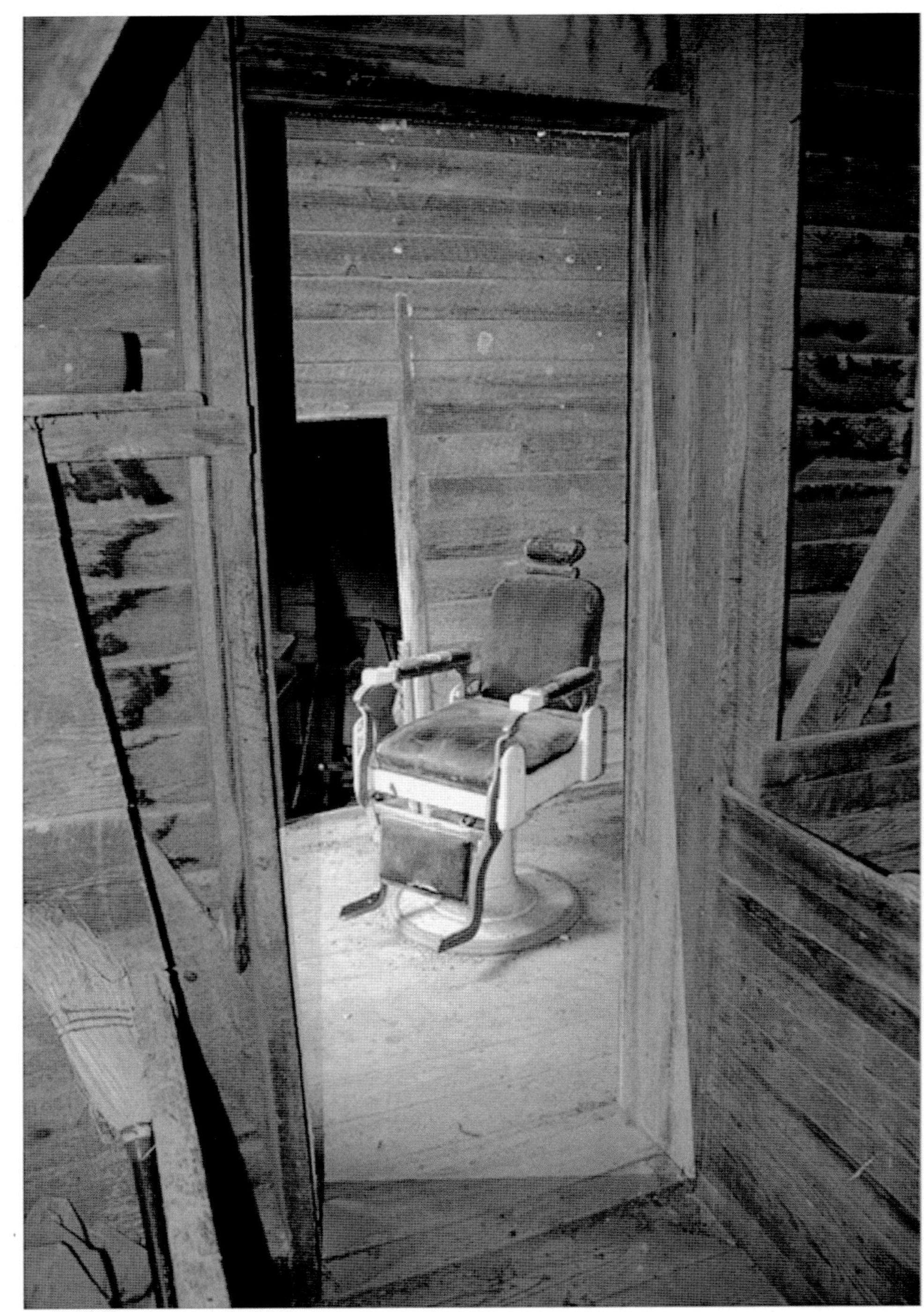

Topaz Mill Barber Shop-Topaz, Missouri

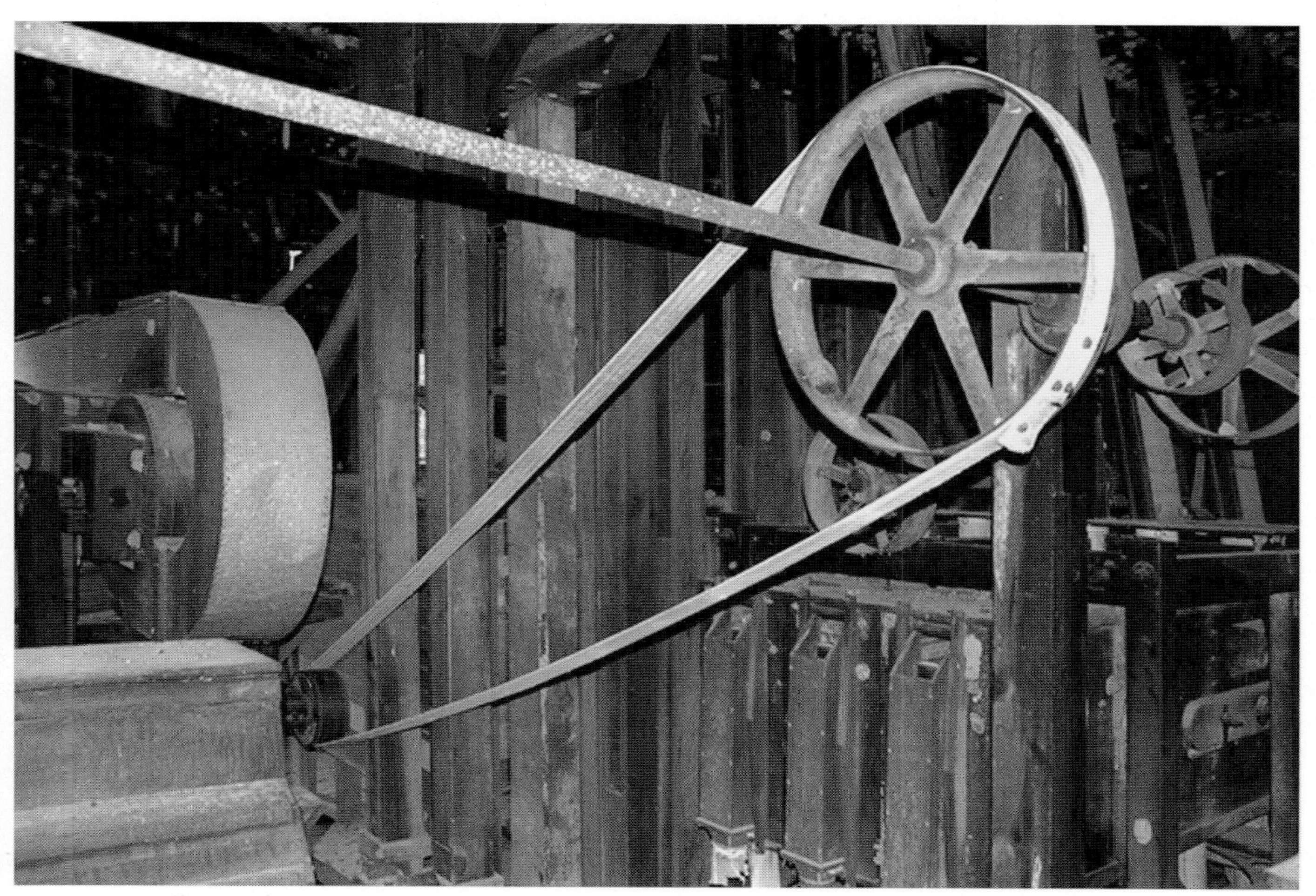

Tcpaz Mill Machinery-Topaz, Missouri

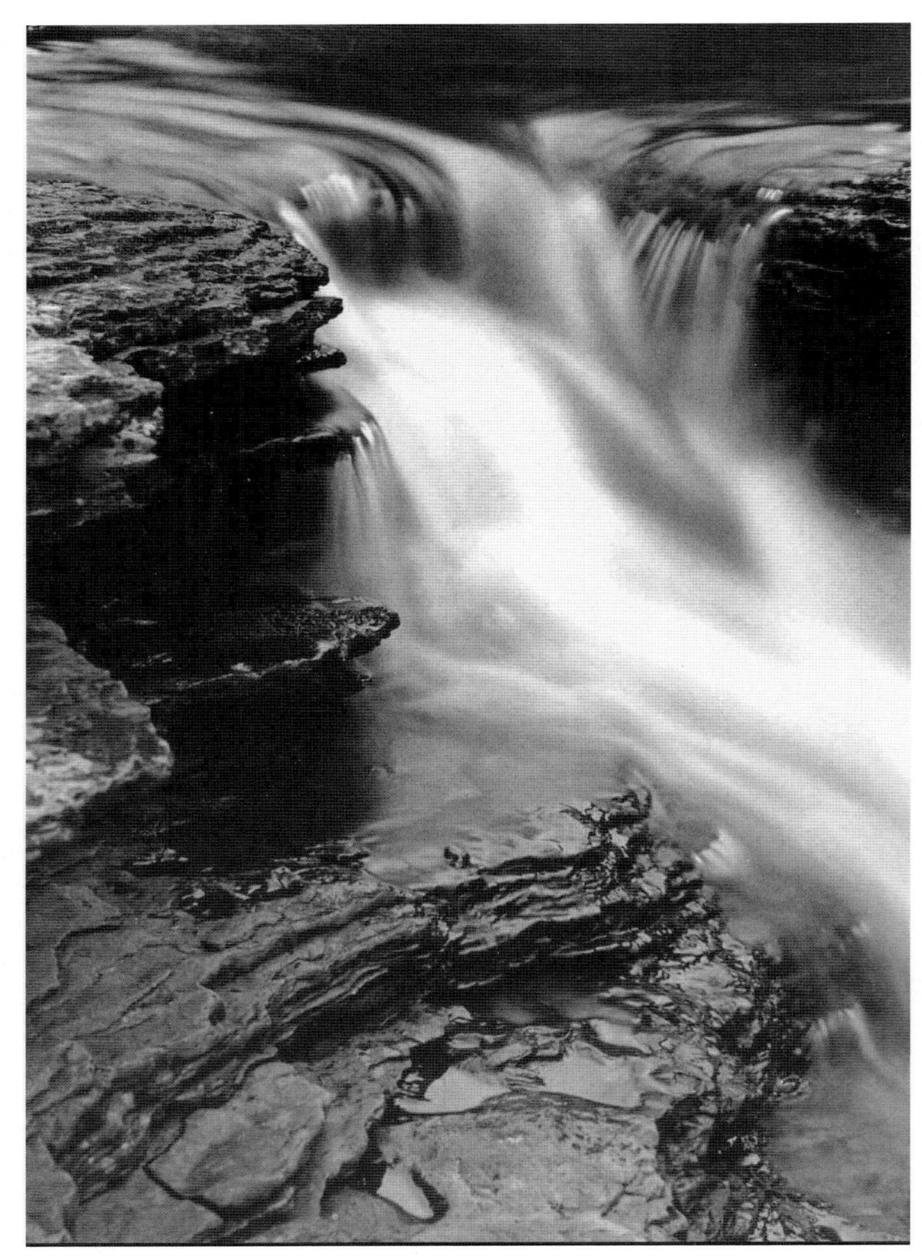

Six Finger Falls on Falling Water Creek near Ben Hur, AR

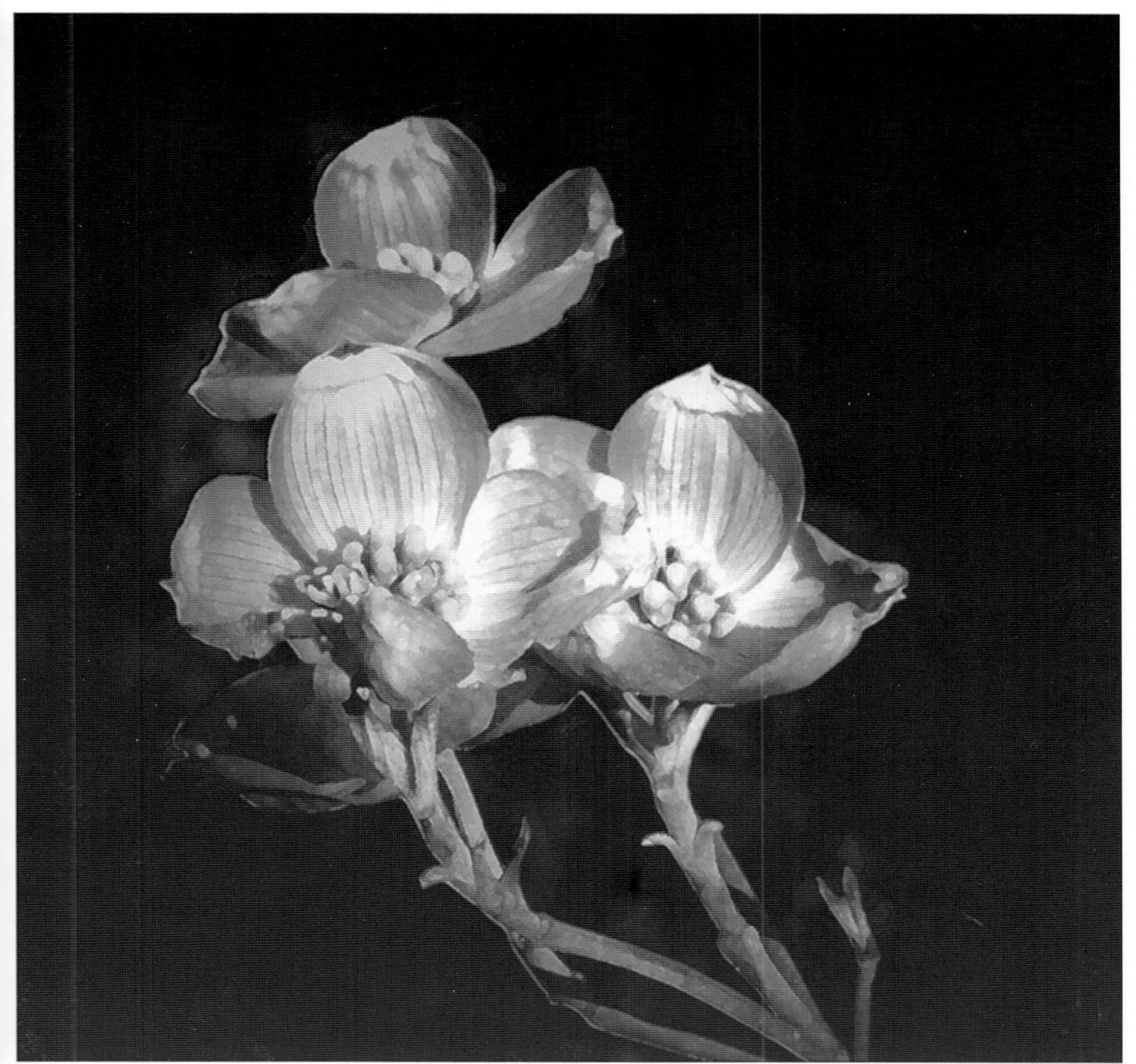
Dogwood Blossoms in Springfield, Missouri

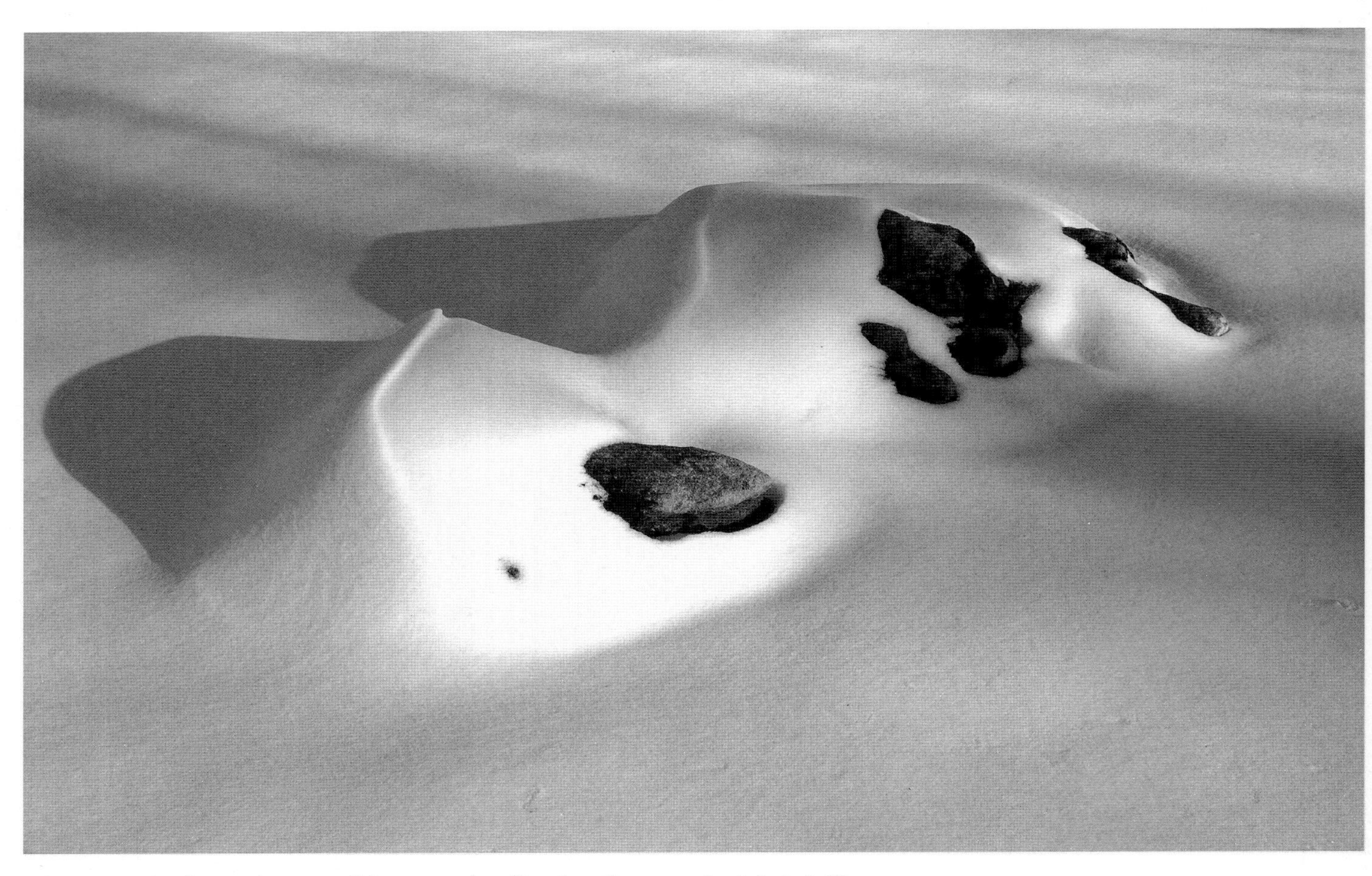

Snow Drifts taken in Fassnight Park-Springfield, MO

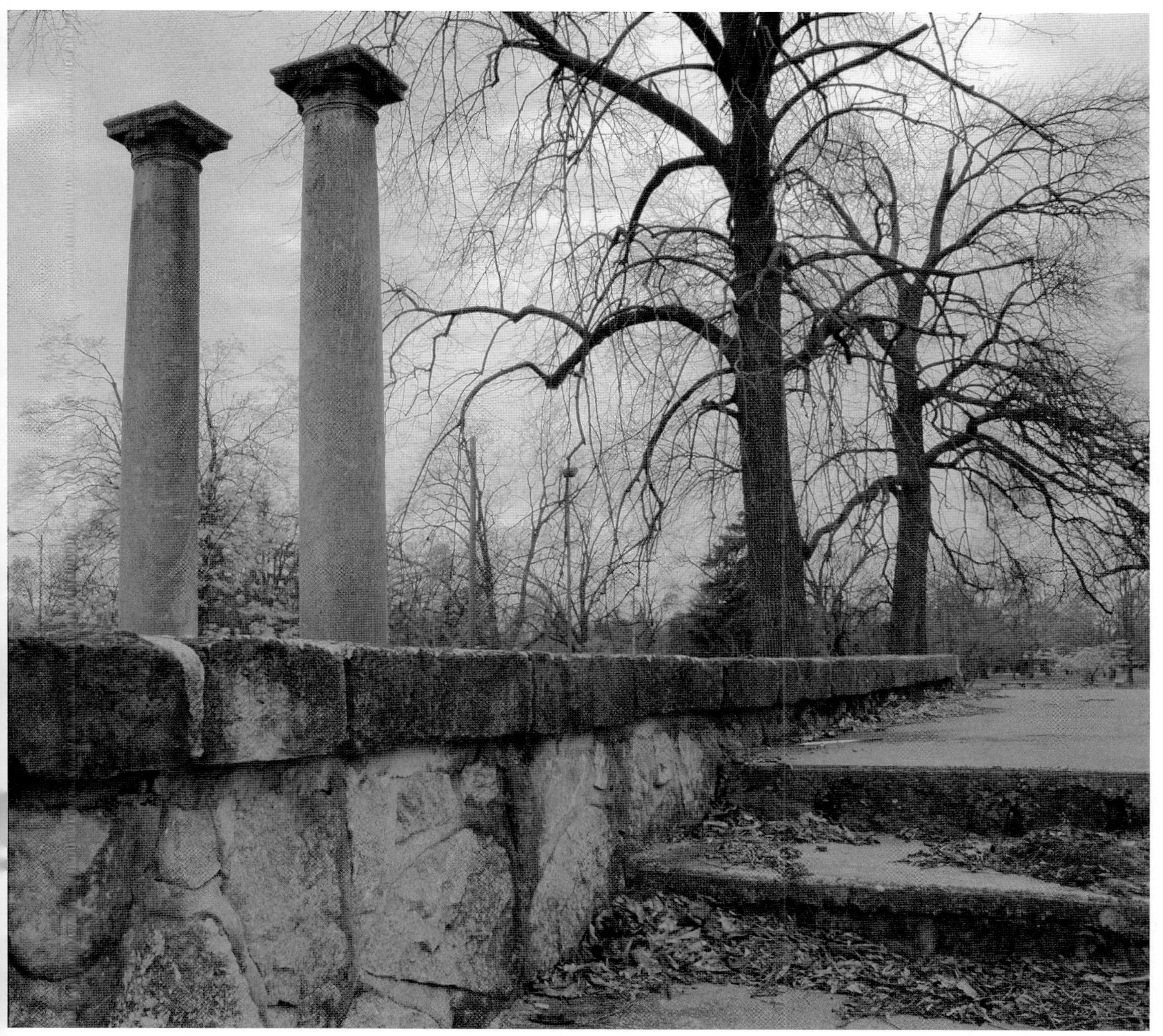

Amphitheater at Phelps Grove Park- Springfield, Missouri

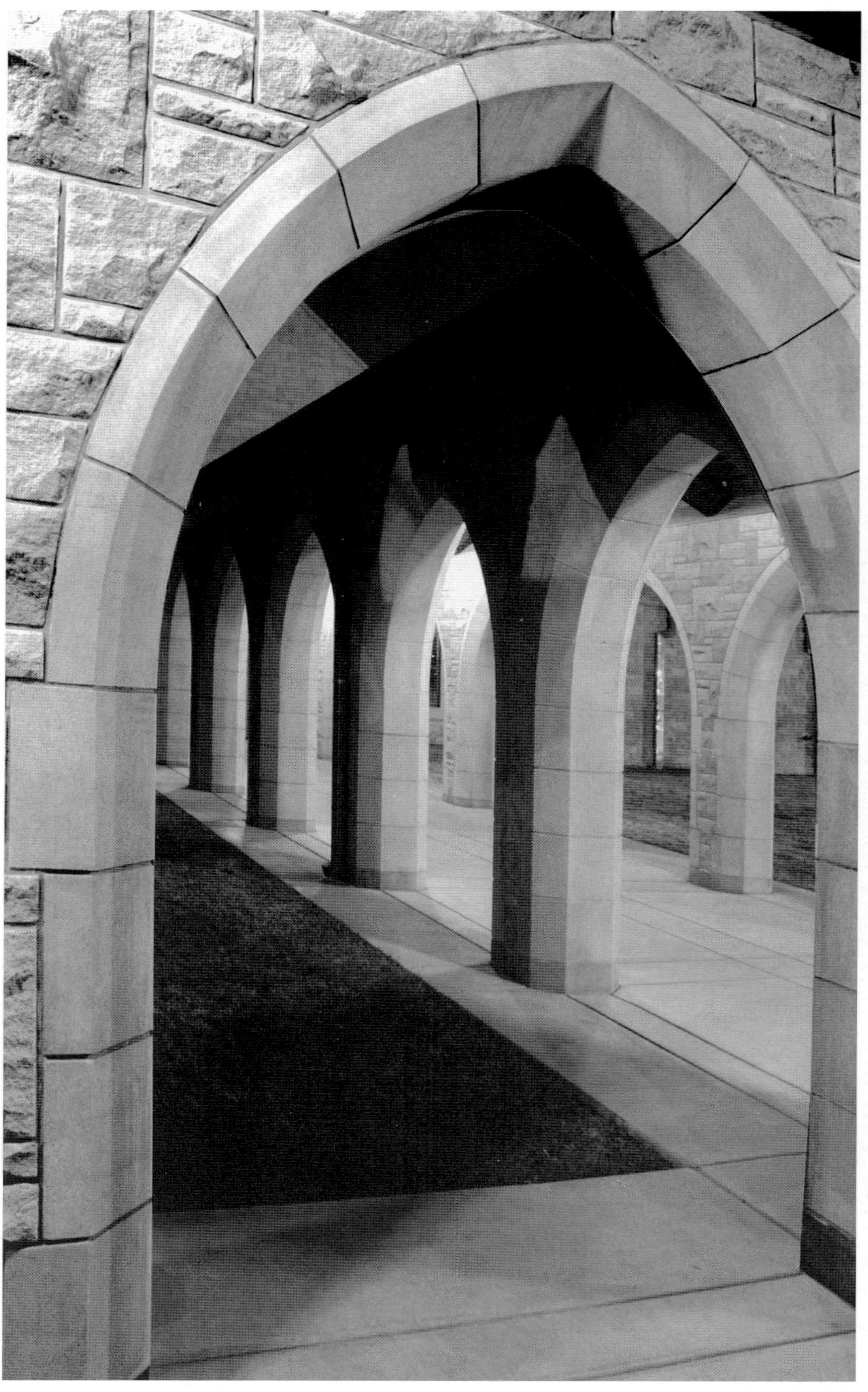

Portico at Christ
Episcopal Church,
Springfield, MO

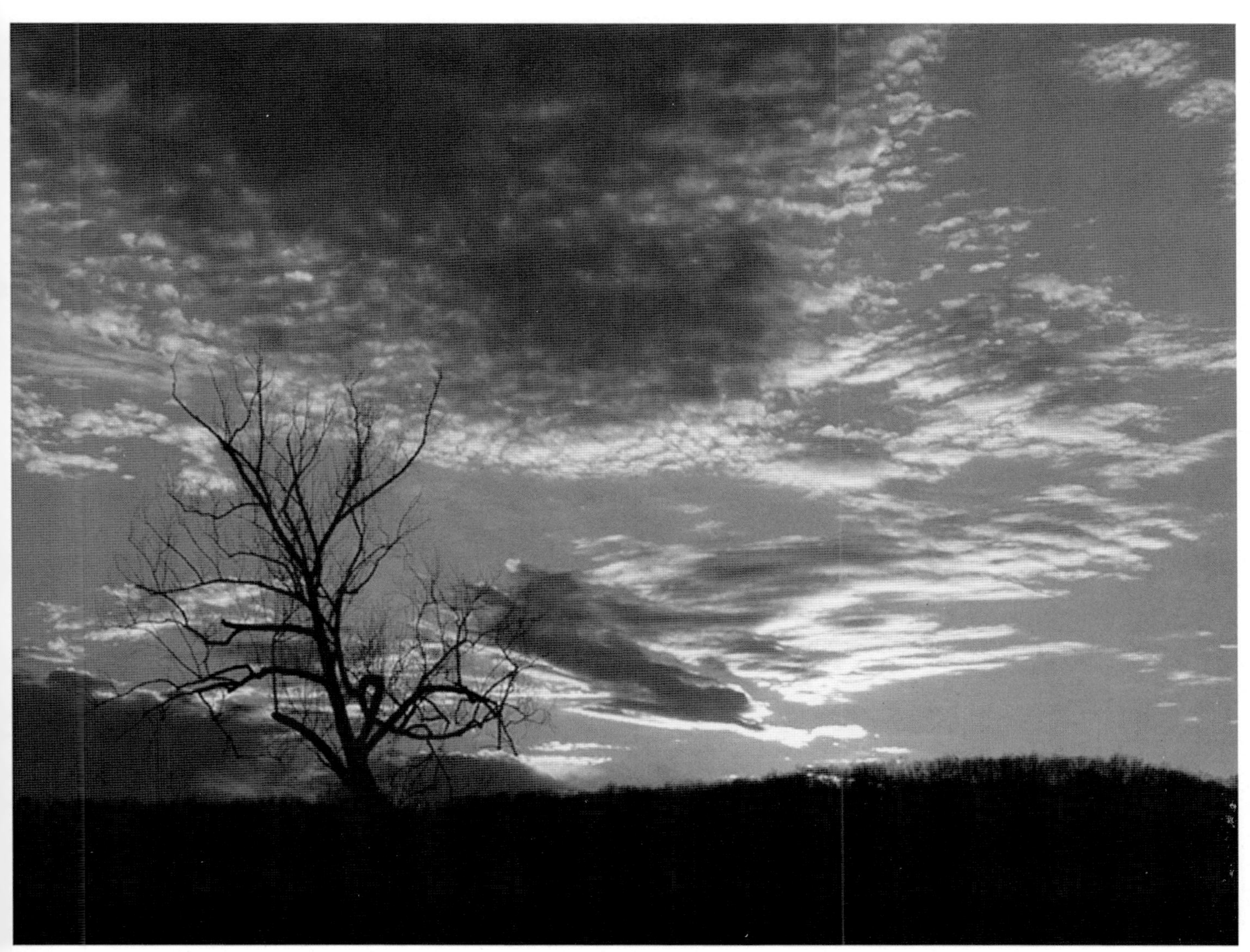

Surset near Forsyth, Missouri

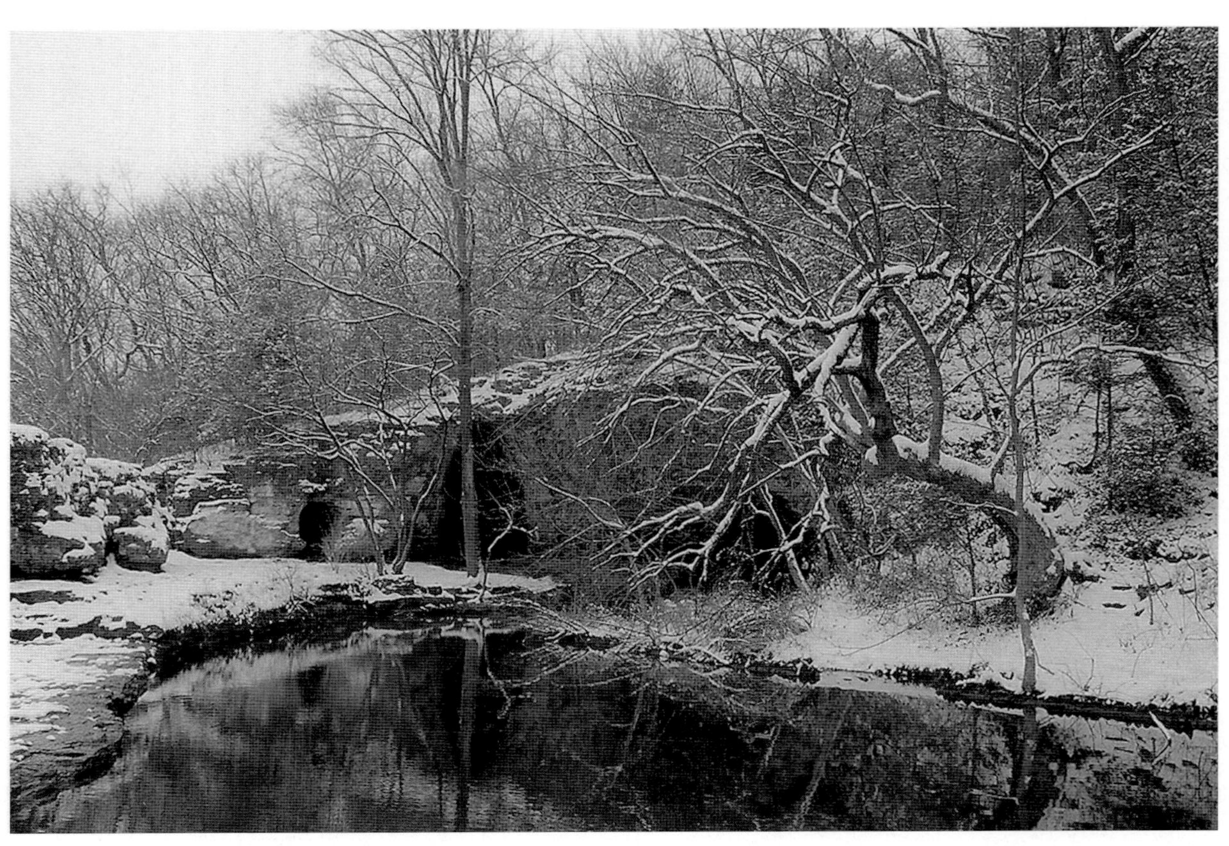

Sequiota Park-Springfield, Missouri

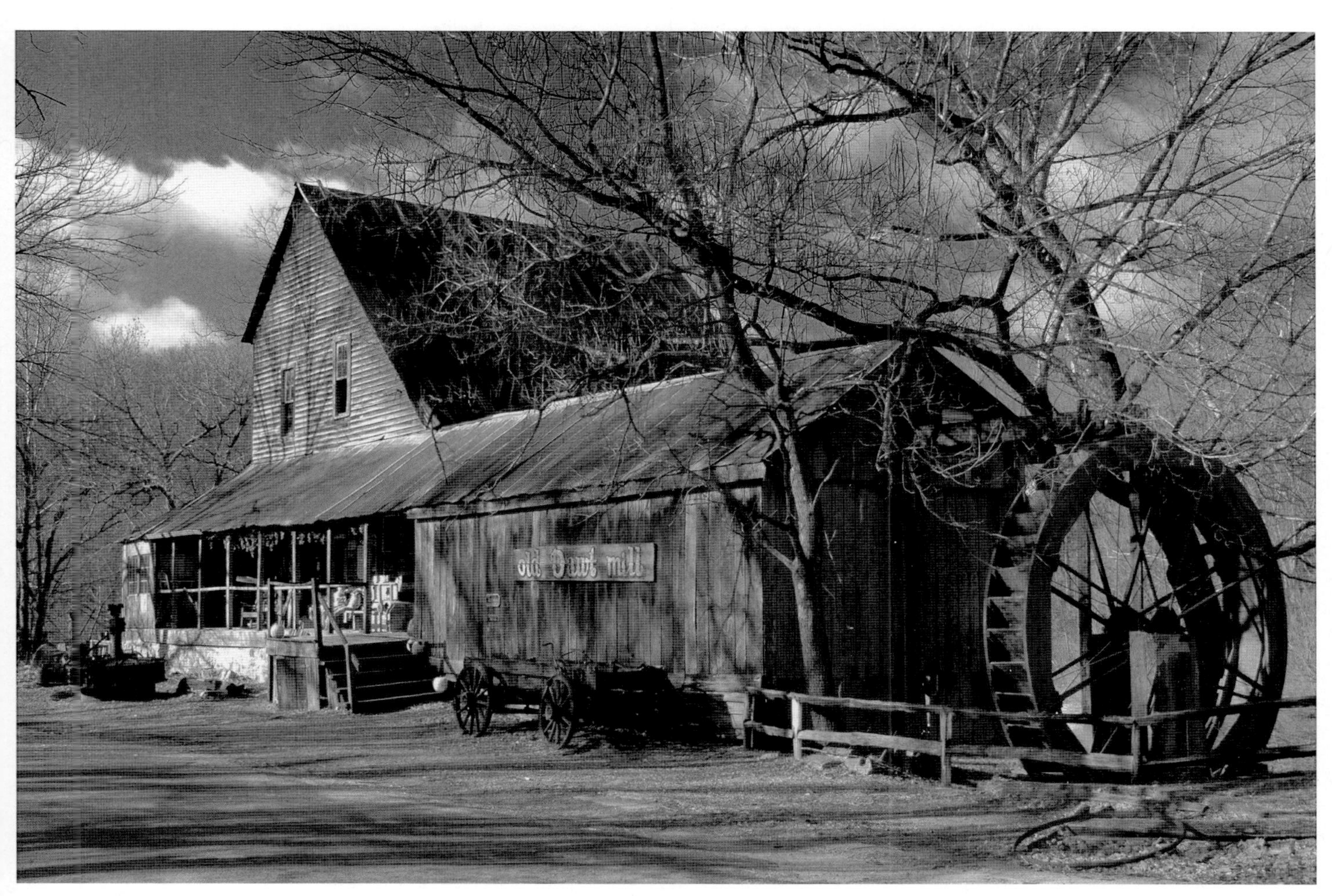

Dawt Mill-Ozark County, Missouri

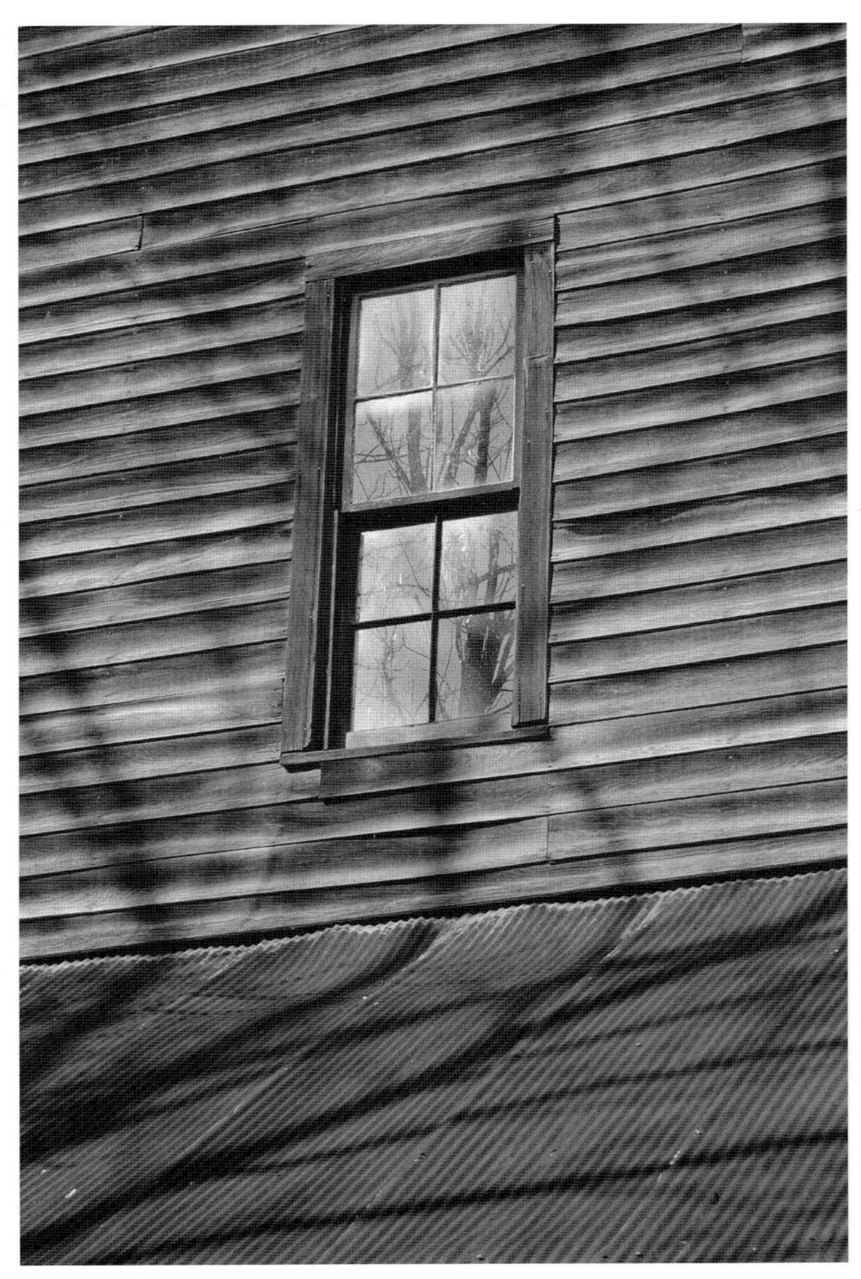

Dawt Mill Window

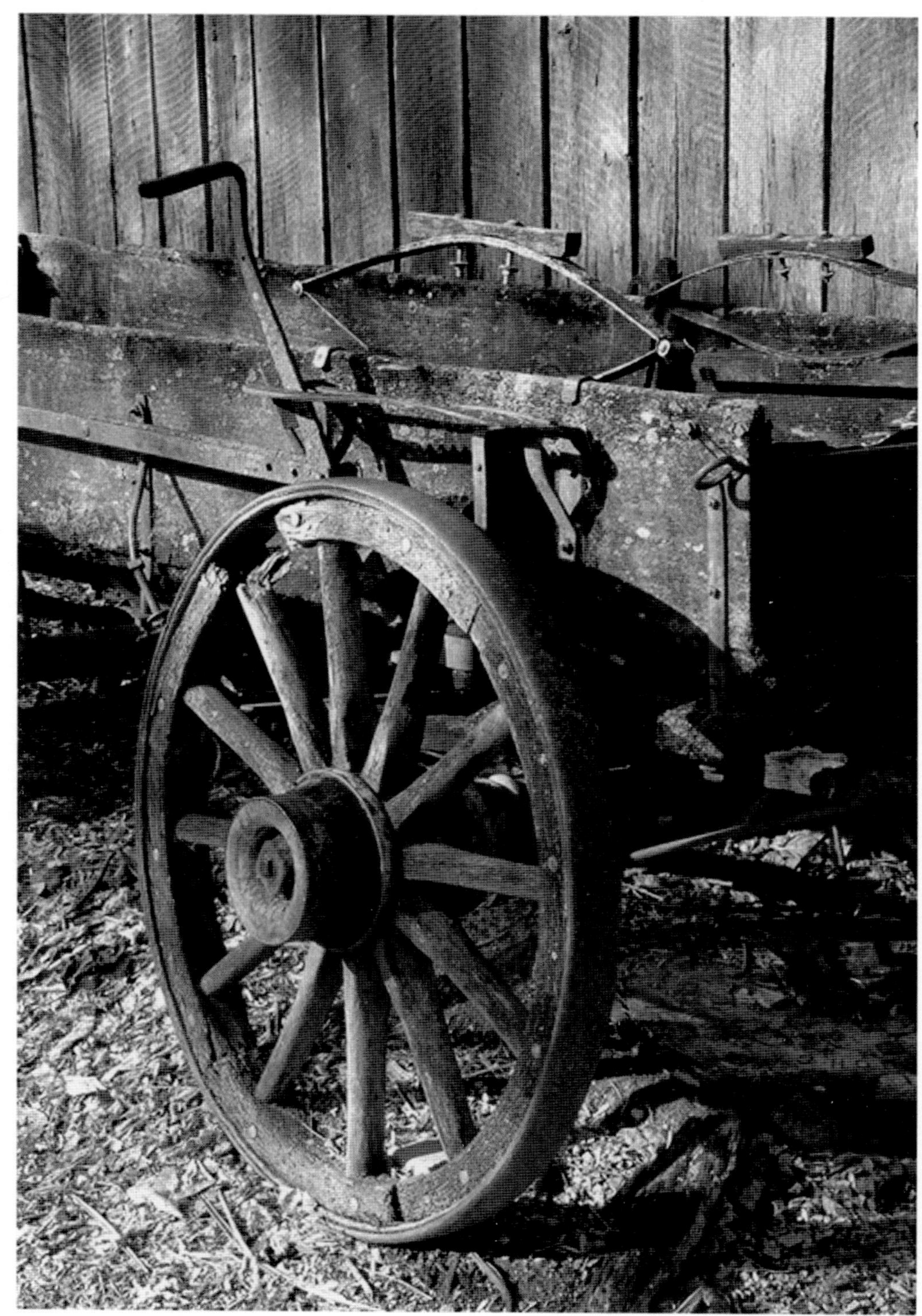

Old Wagon at Dawt Mill in Ozark County, Missouri

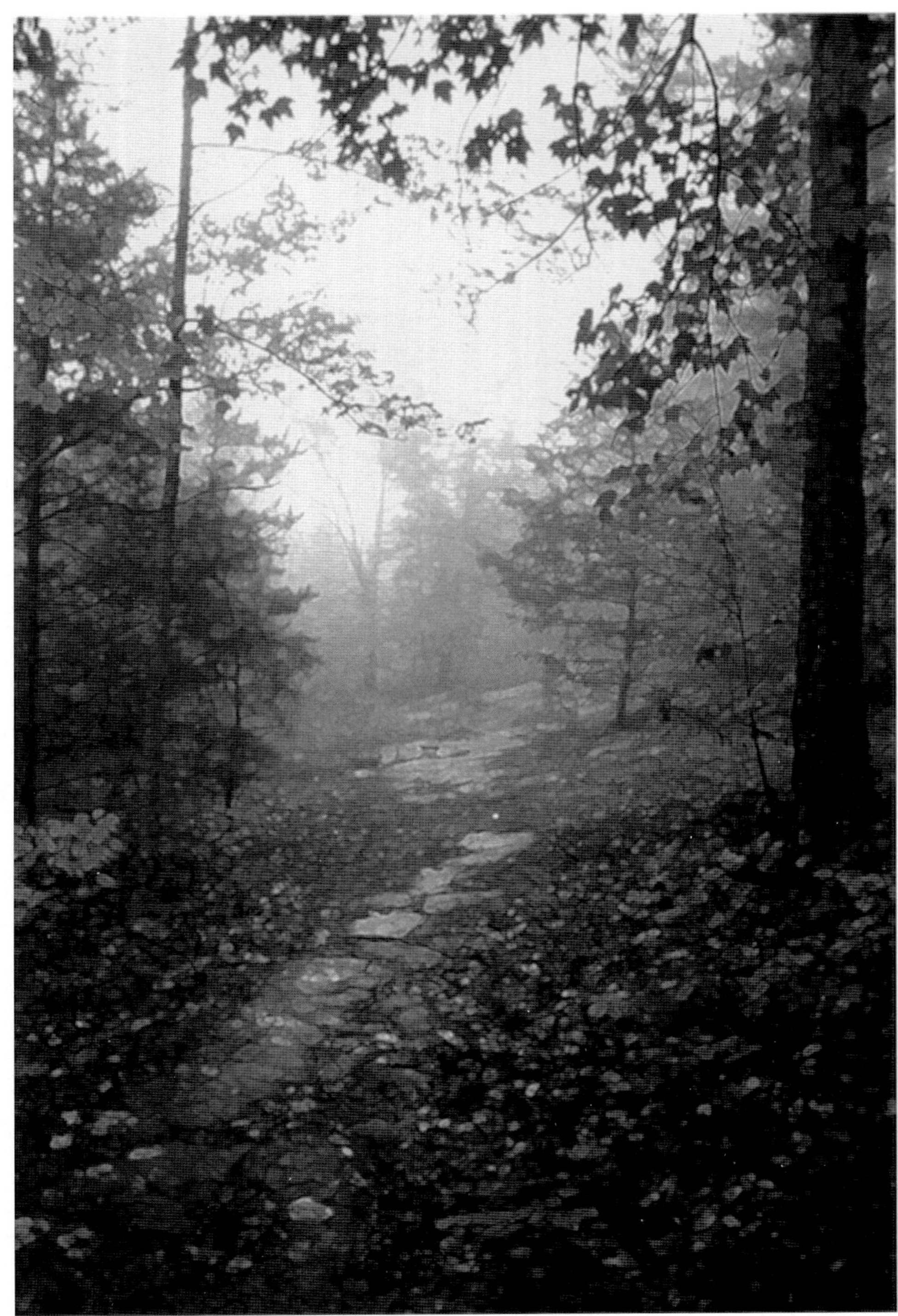

SOLITUDE

Fear like smoke choking
my breath, loneliness and
self-doubt nipping at my
heels like a hound-plagued
stag I flee

Down the fog-shrouded
path where trees bend their
dew-laden boughs in
empathy beckoning me on
relentlessly

To disappear into the
selfless mist where nature's
singular purpose of
directing the un-ending
symphony

Of birth, life, death and
renewal is played with creative
abandonment upon the
fathomless stage of
time.

Carl James

Boen Gulf-Upper Buffalo
Wilderness Area

Hwy. #181 near
Zanoni in Ozark
County, Missouri

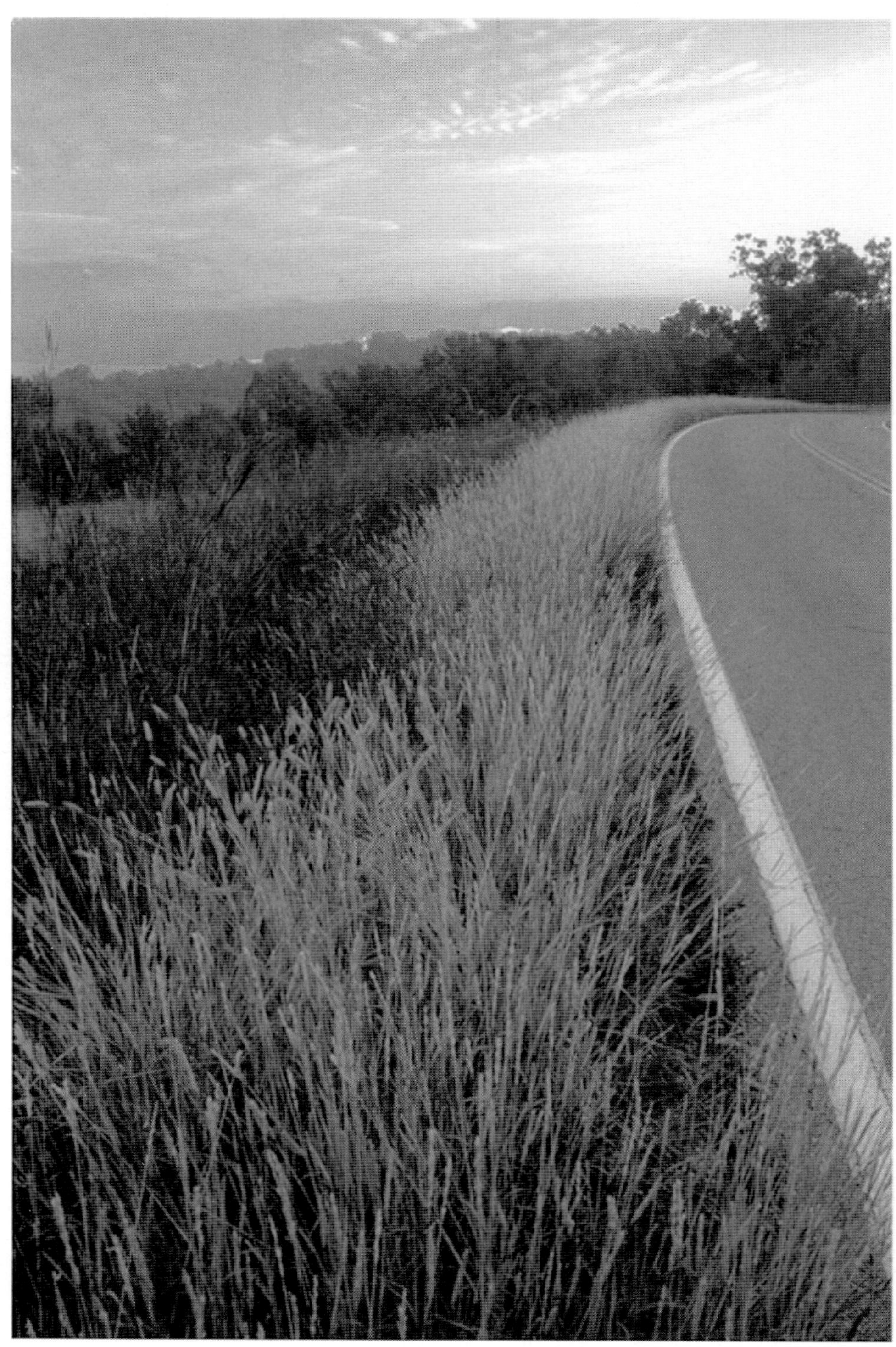

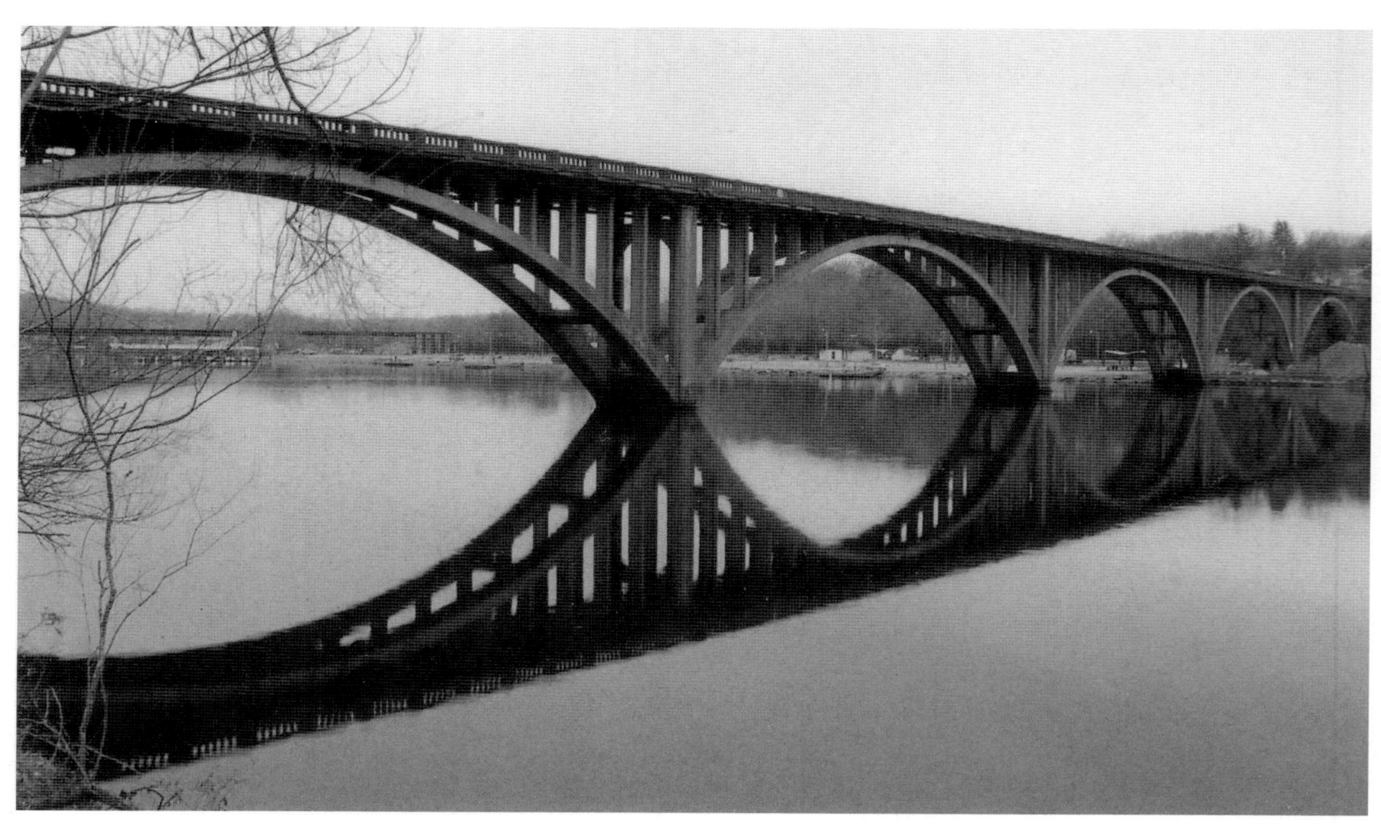

Hwy. #76 Bridge across Lake Taneycomo, Branson, Missouri

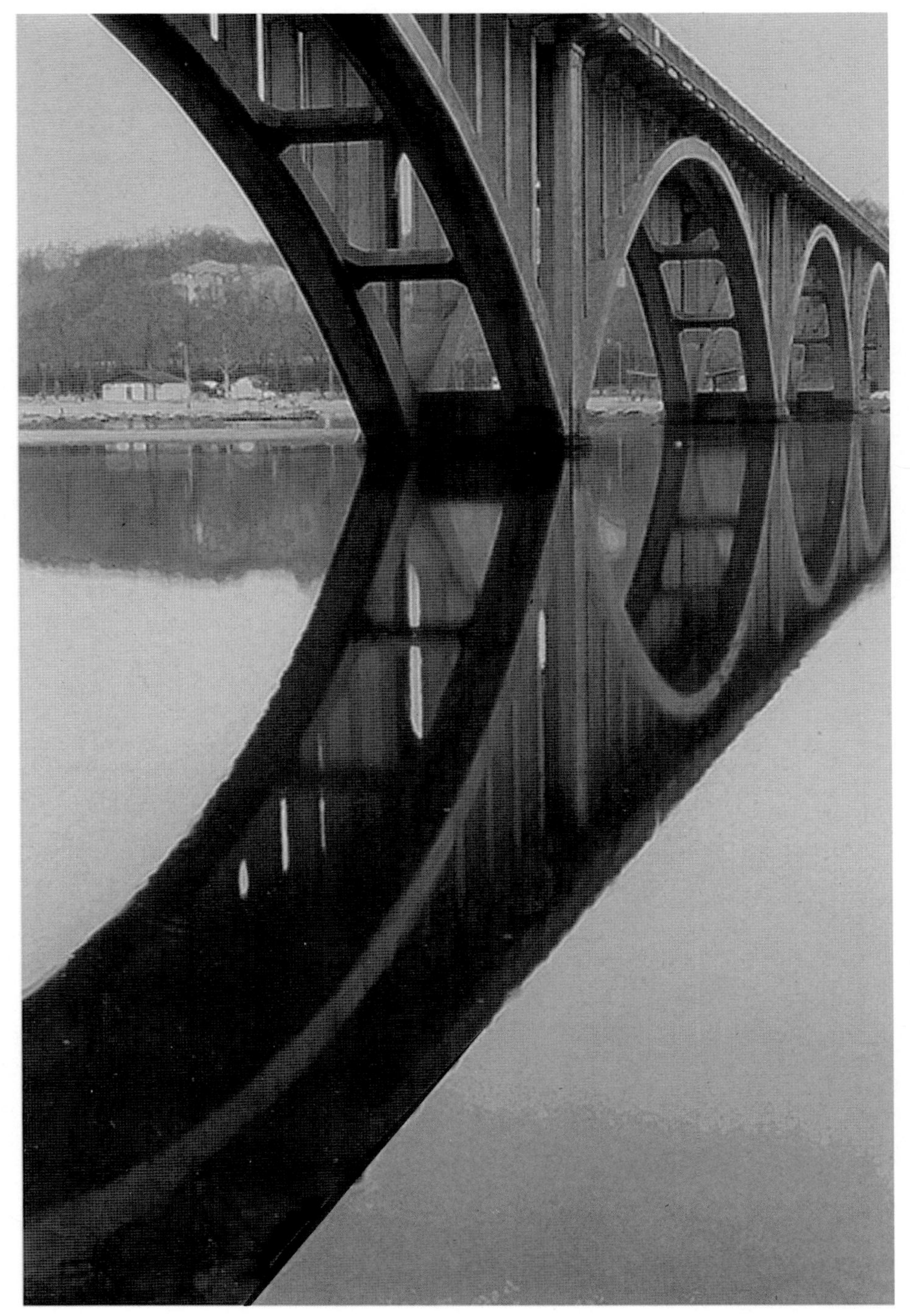

Hwy. #76 Bridge crossing Lake Taneycomo near Branson, Missouri

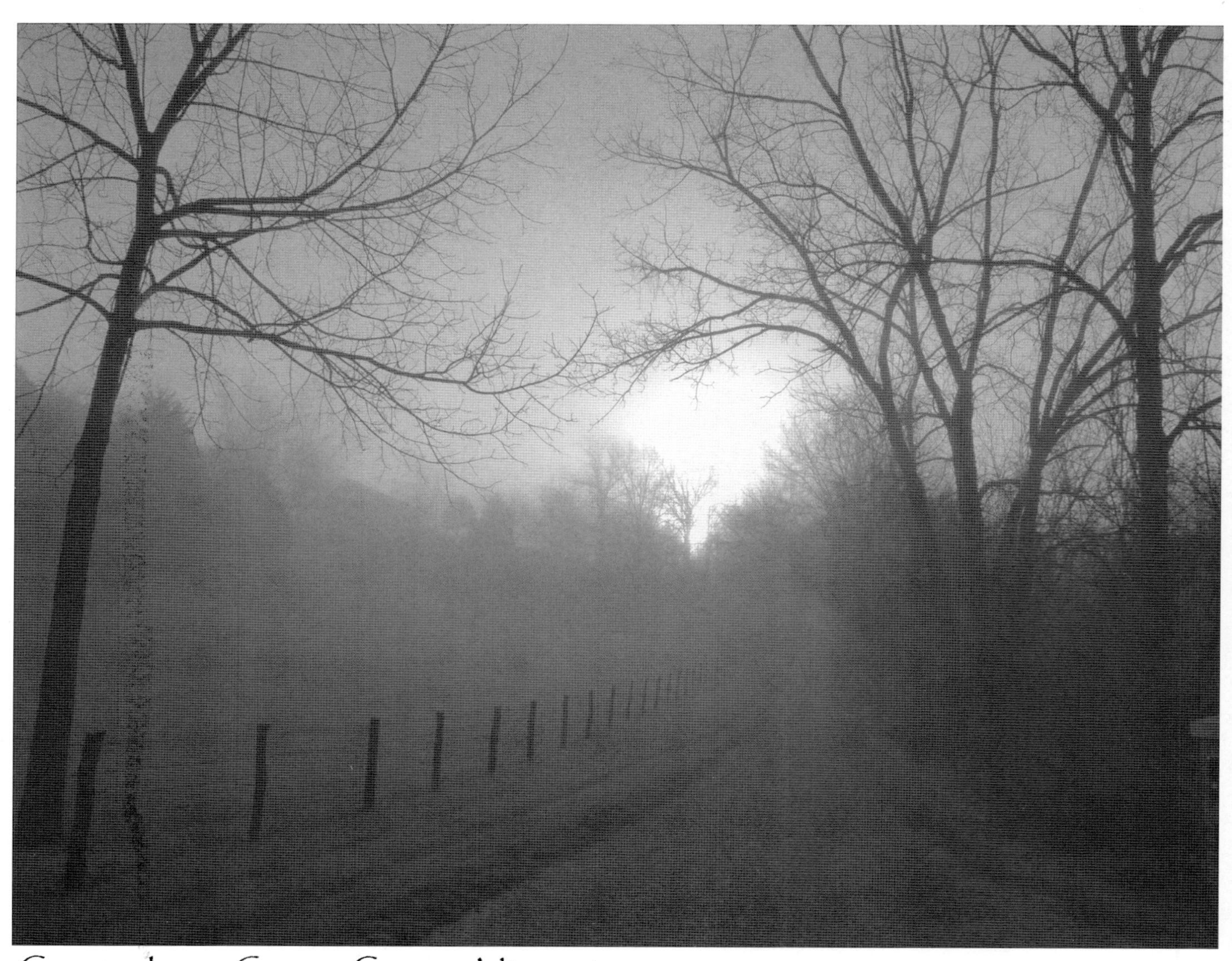

Country Lane-Greene County, Missouri

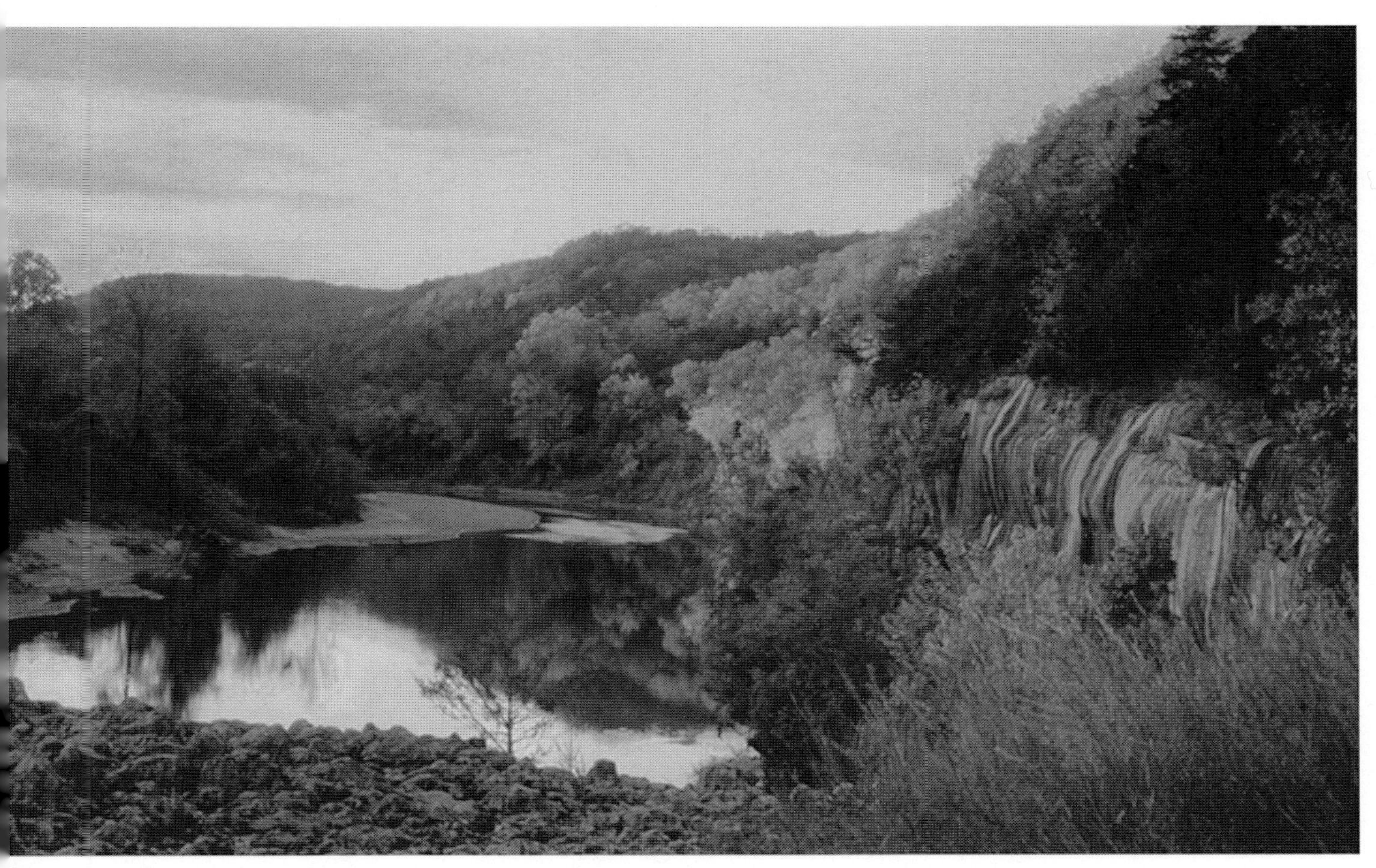

Buffalo Point State Park near Yellville, Arkansas

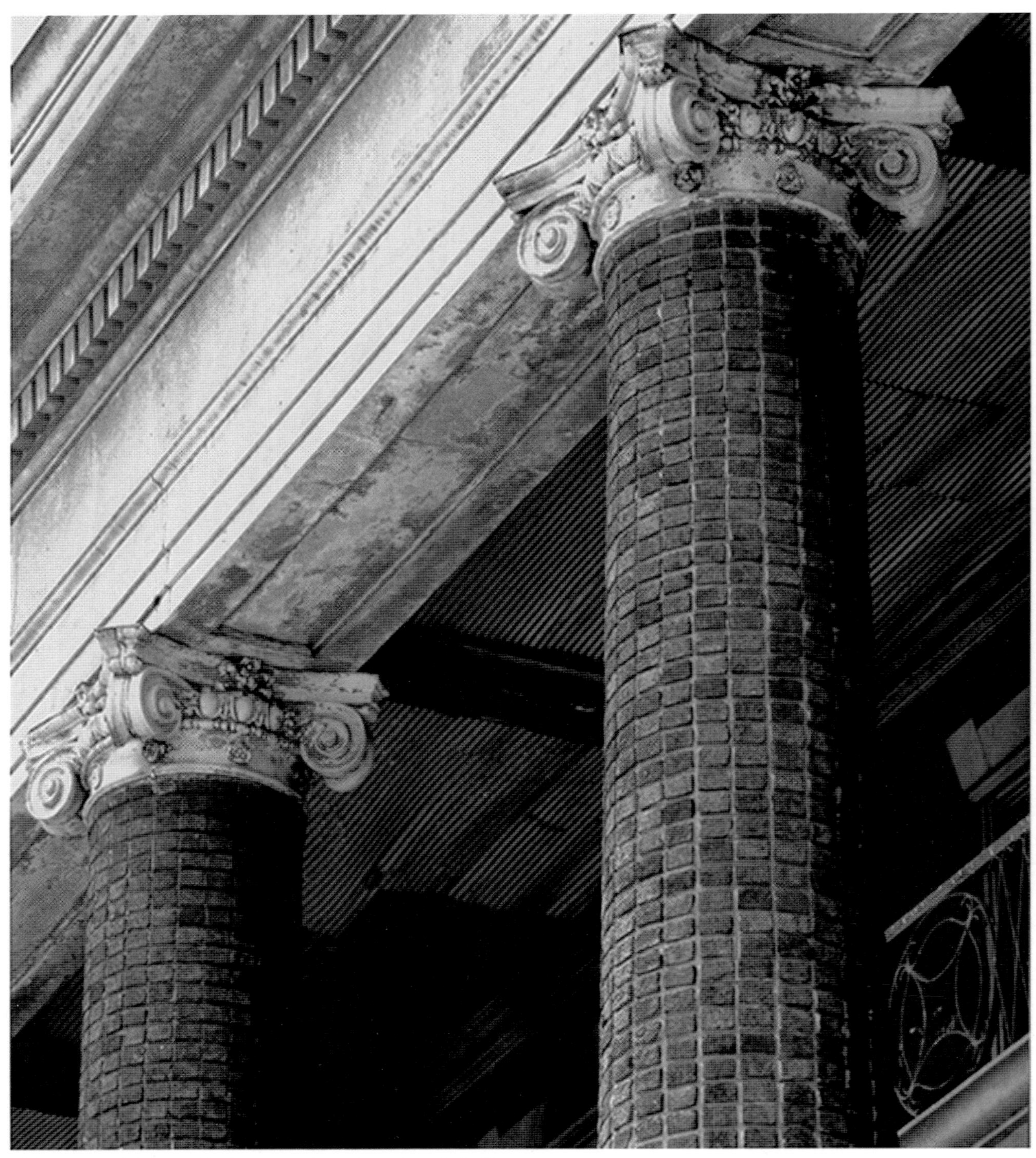

Old Building Colonnade-Joplin, MO

The Shroud of Winter

Maple Park Cemetery Springfield, MO

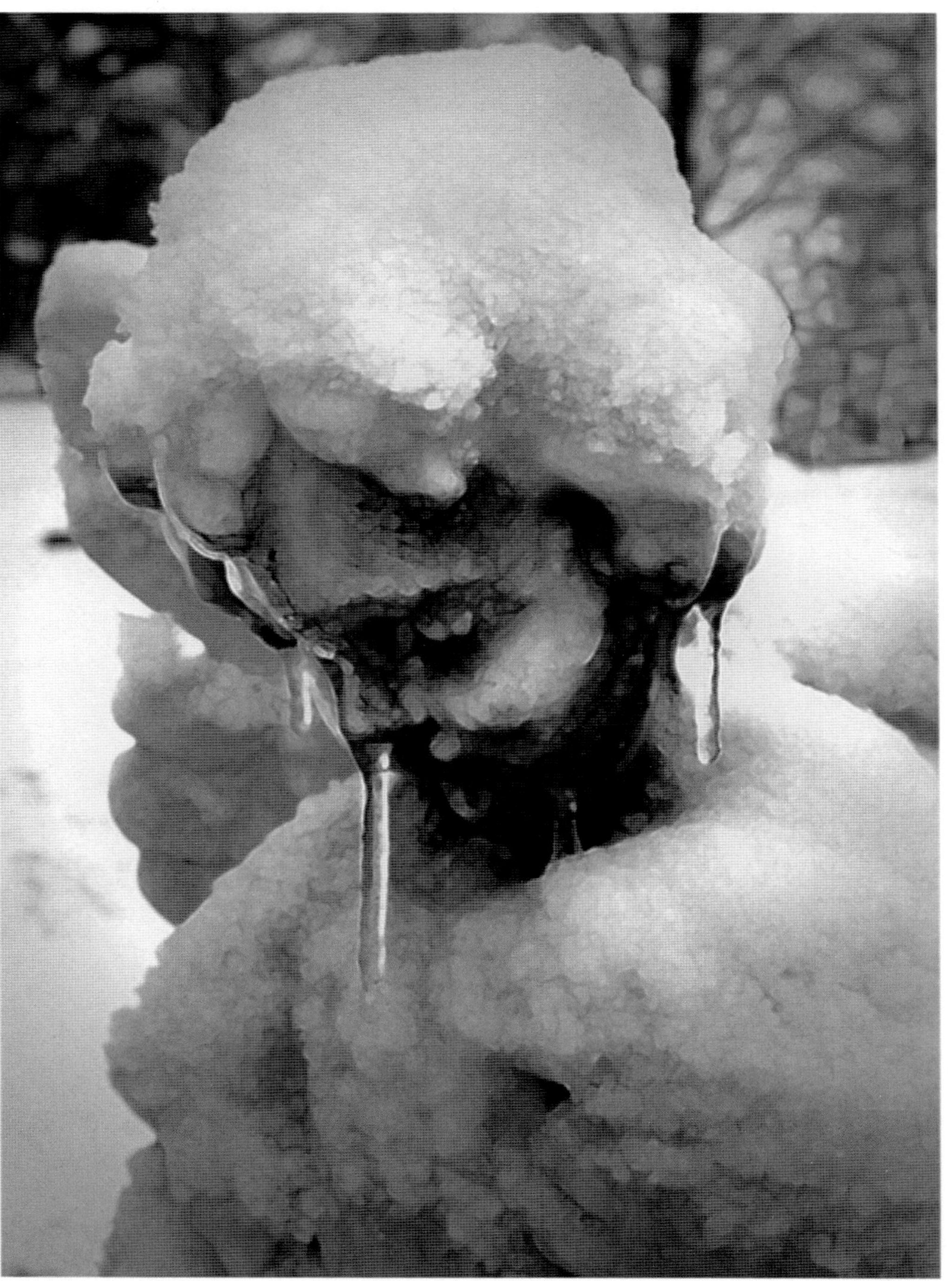

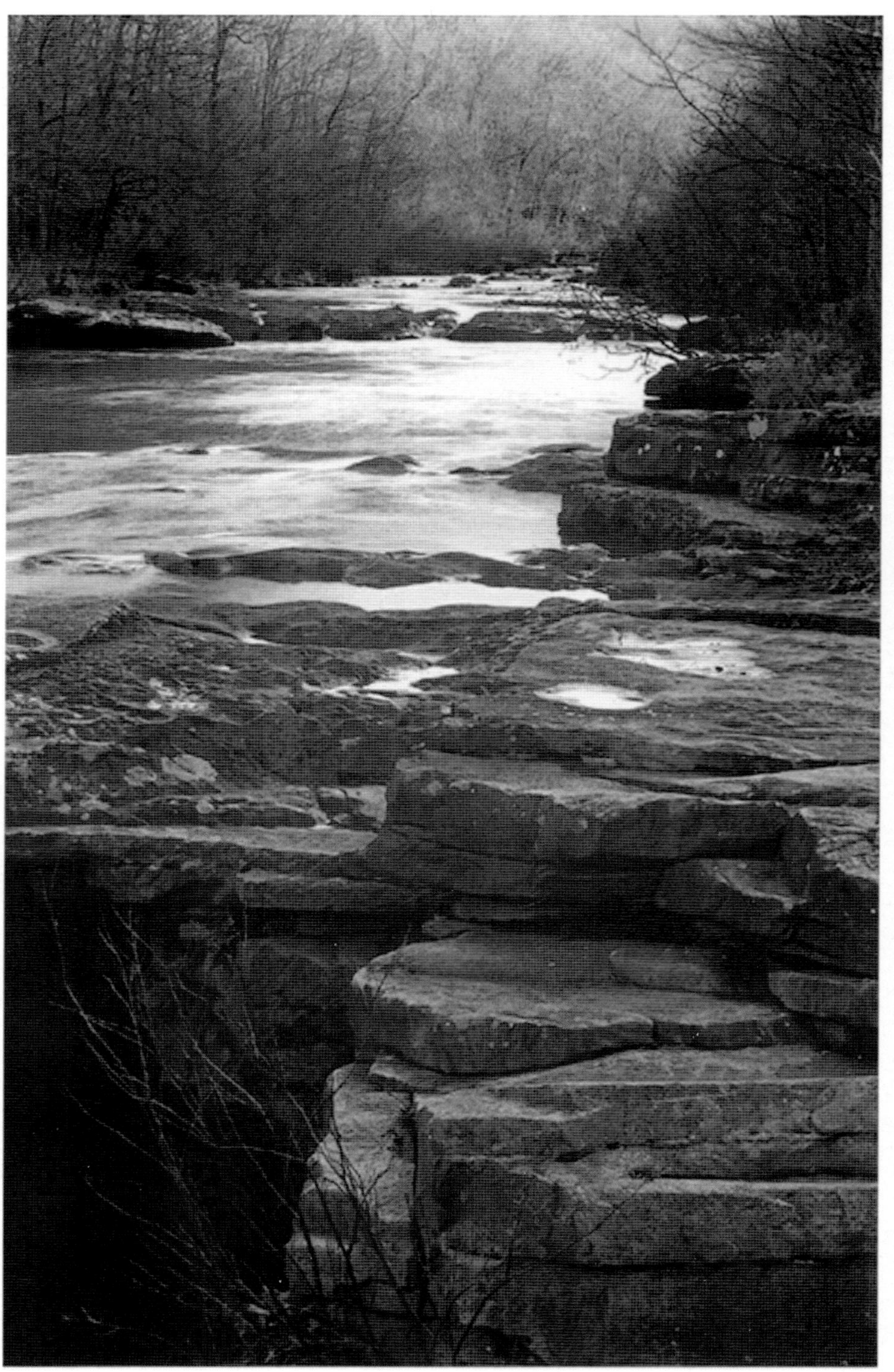

Falling Water Creek
near Mossville, AR

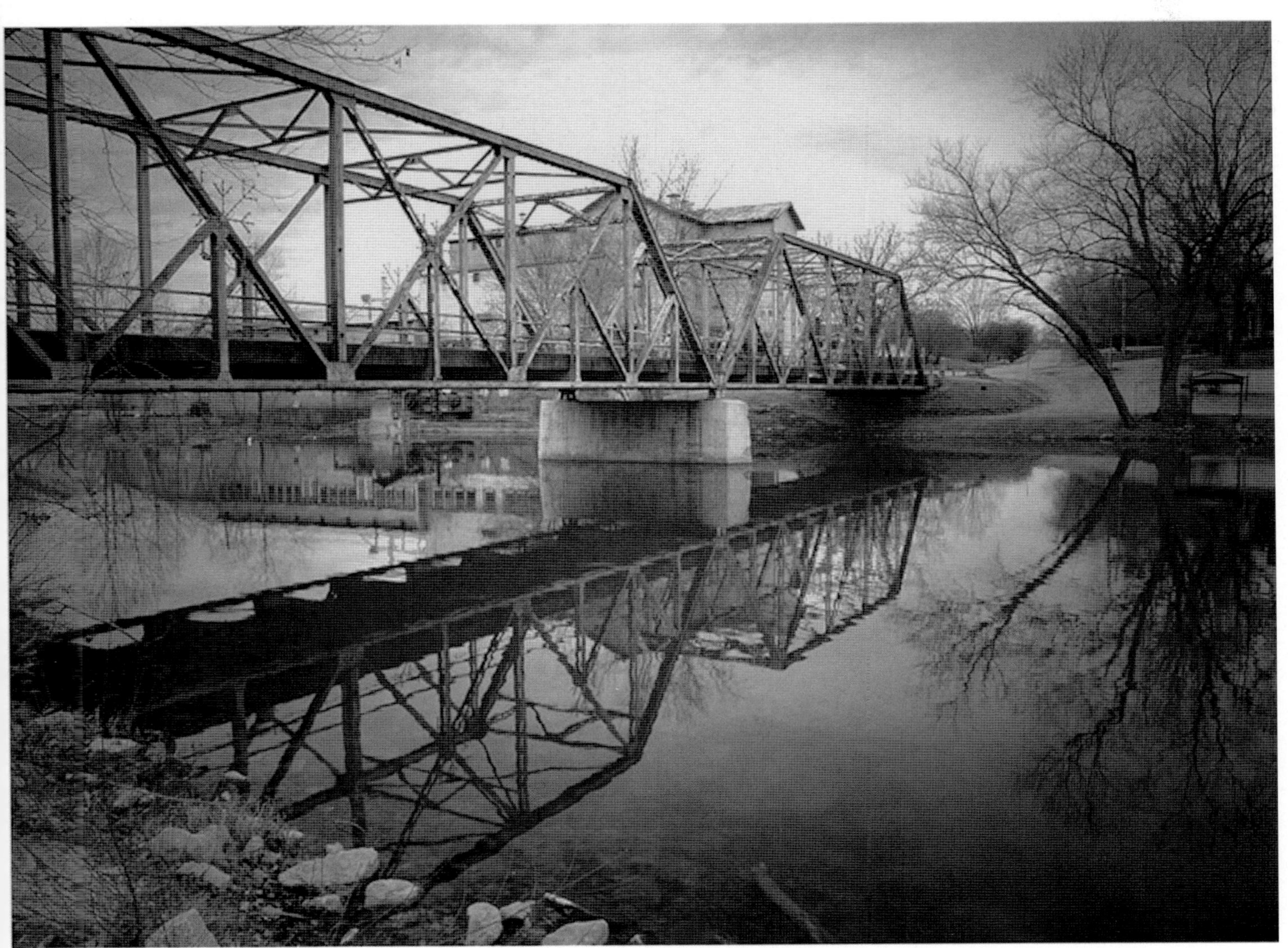

Finley River Bridge, Dam, Mill & Mill Pond-Ozark, Missouri

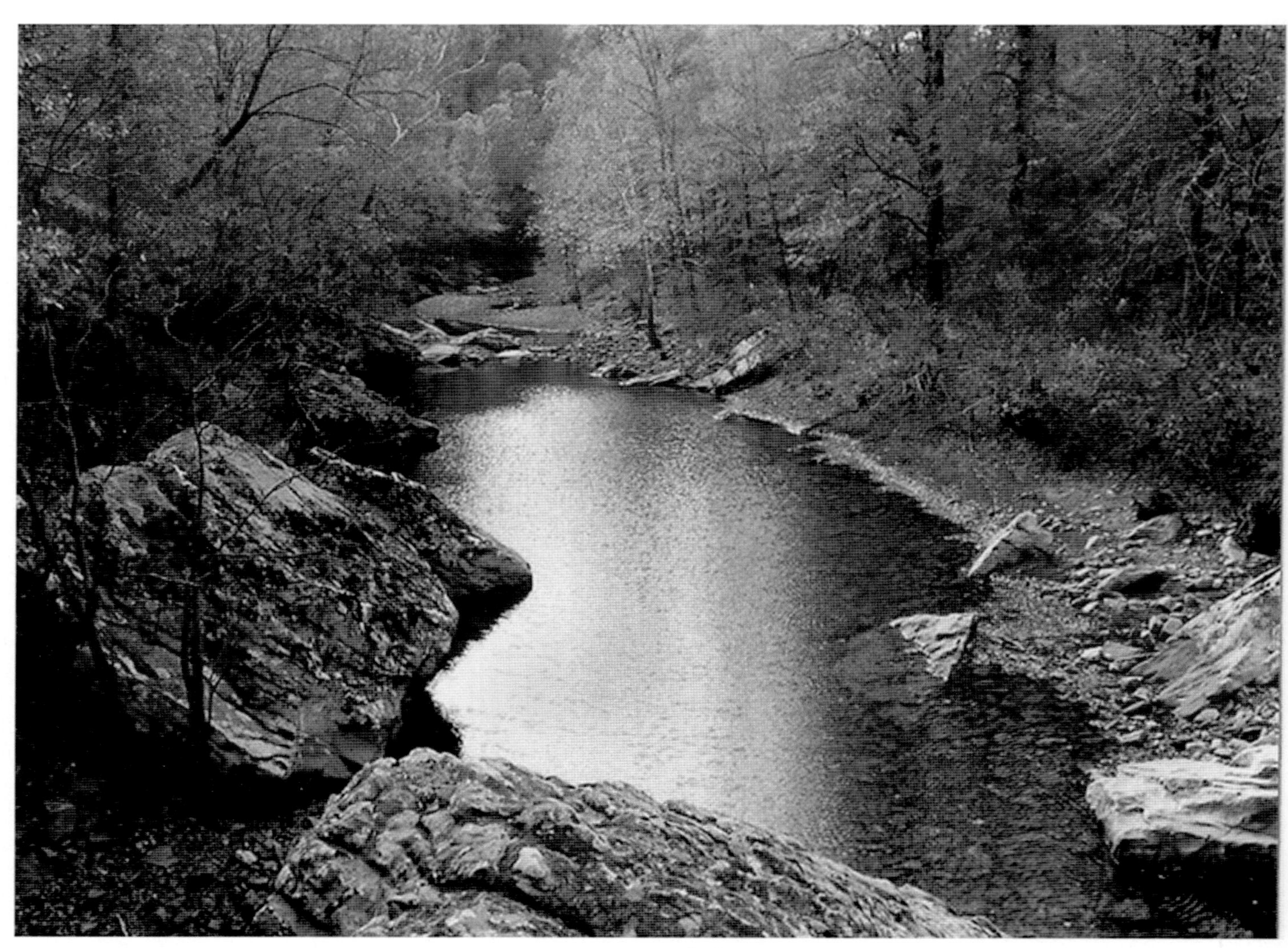

The Hailstones of the Upper Buffalo River - Arkansas

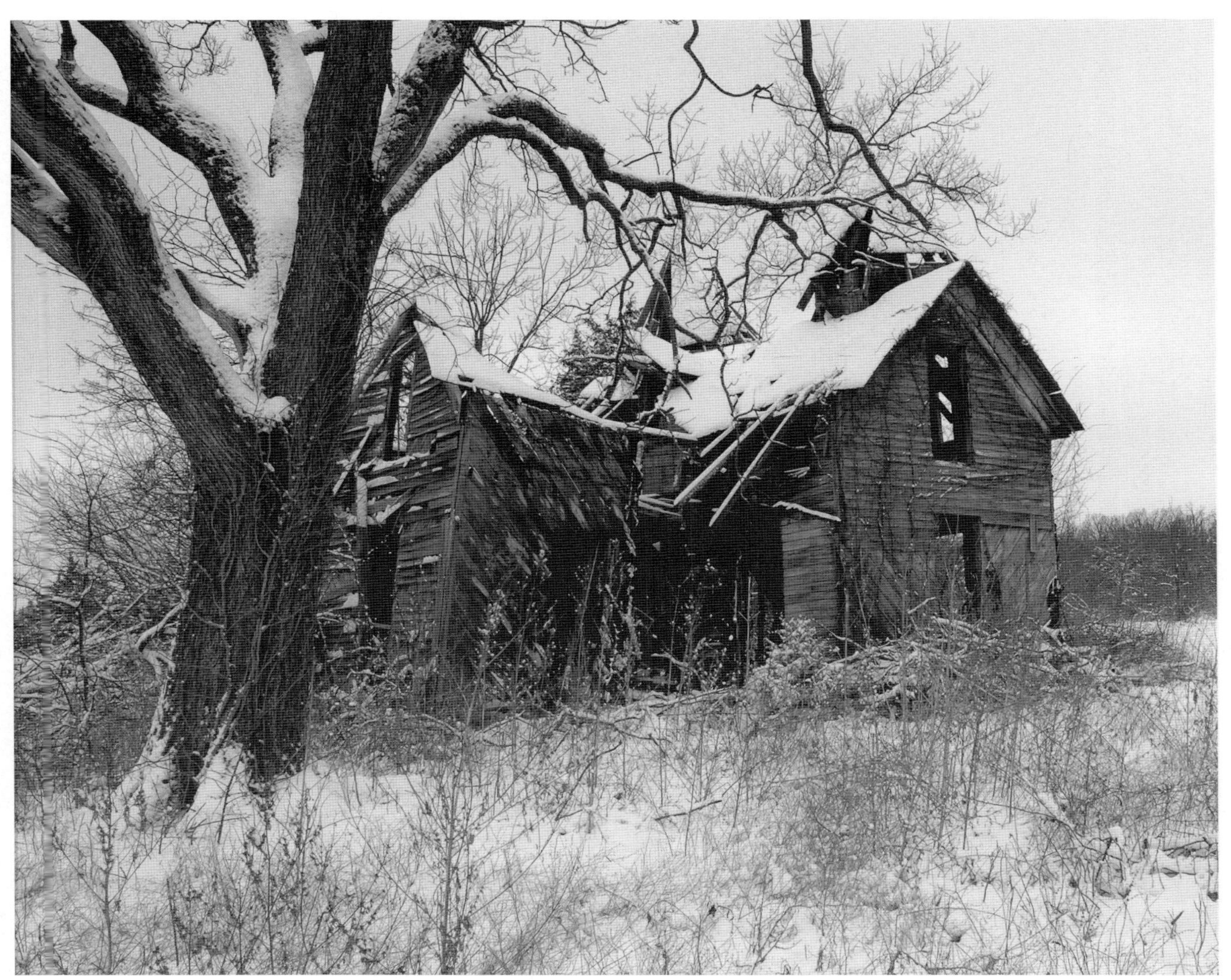

Abandoned House near Pleasant Hope, Missouri

Old Abandoned House
near Pleasant Hope, MO

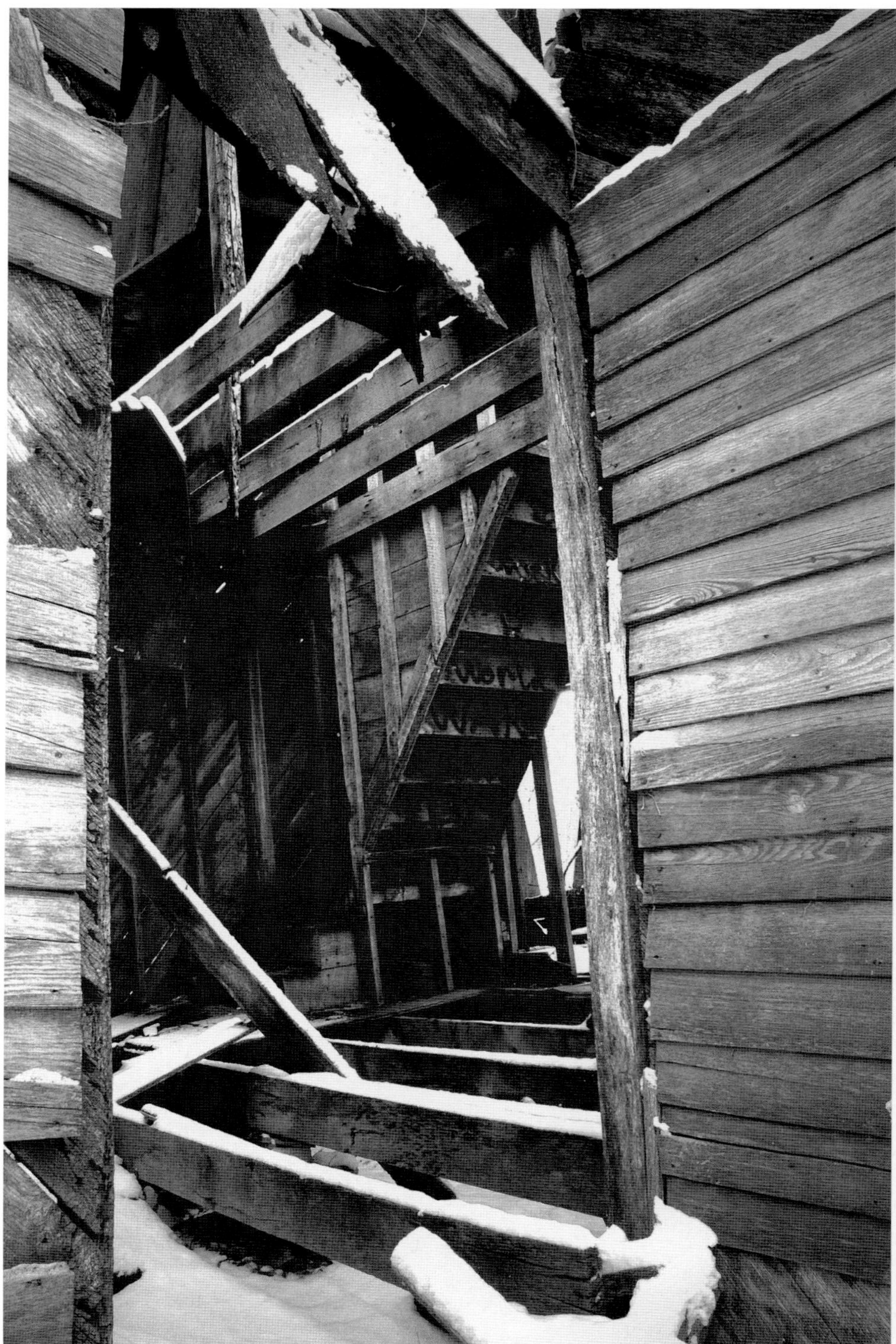

Beauty can be found in all things born of the natural process of nature's reclamation of her elements back into herself

Carl James

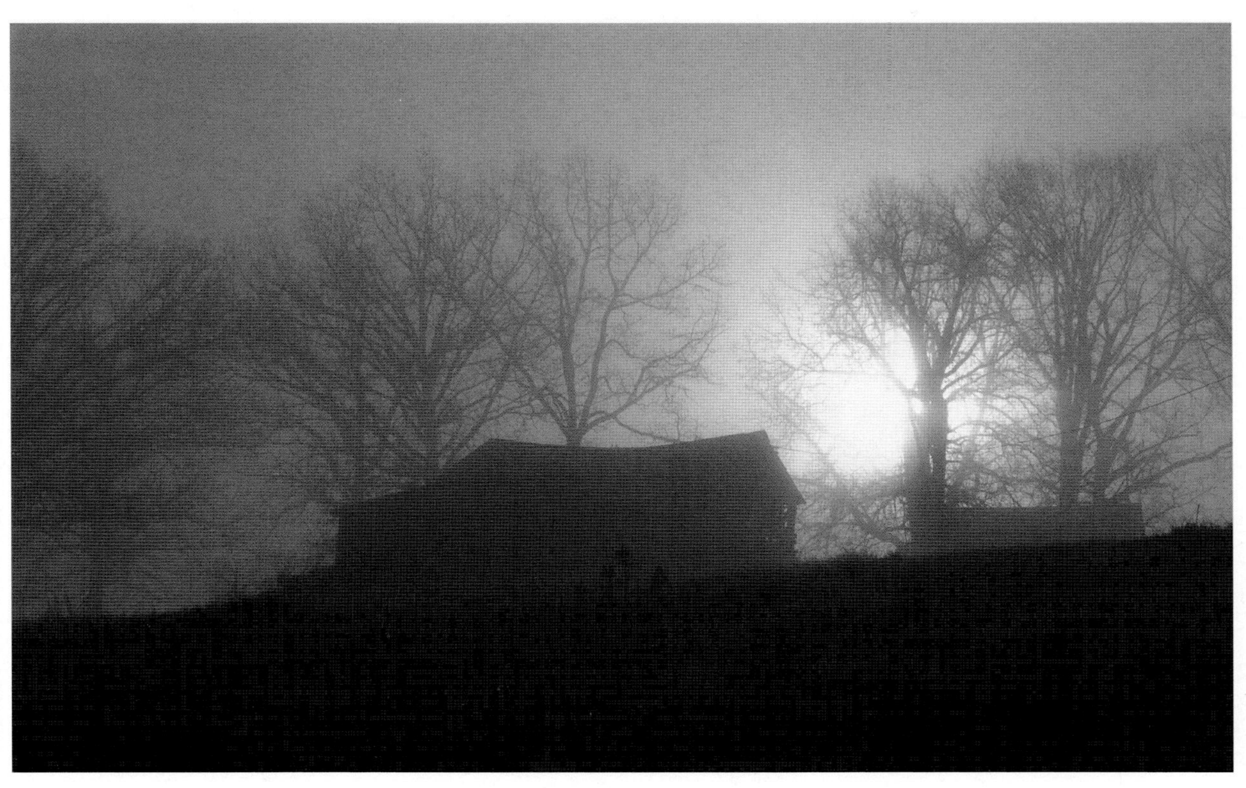

Along Farm Road #192-Greene County, Missouri

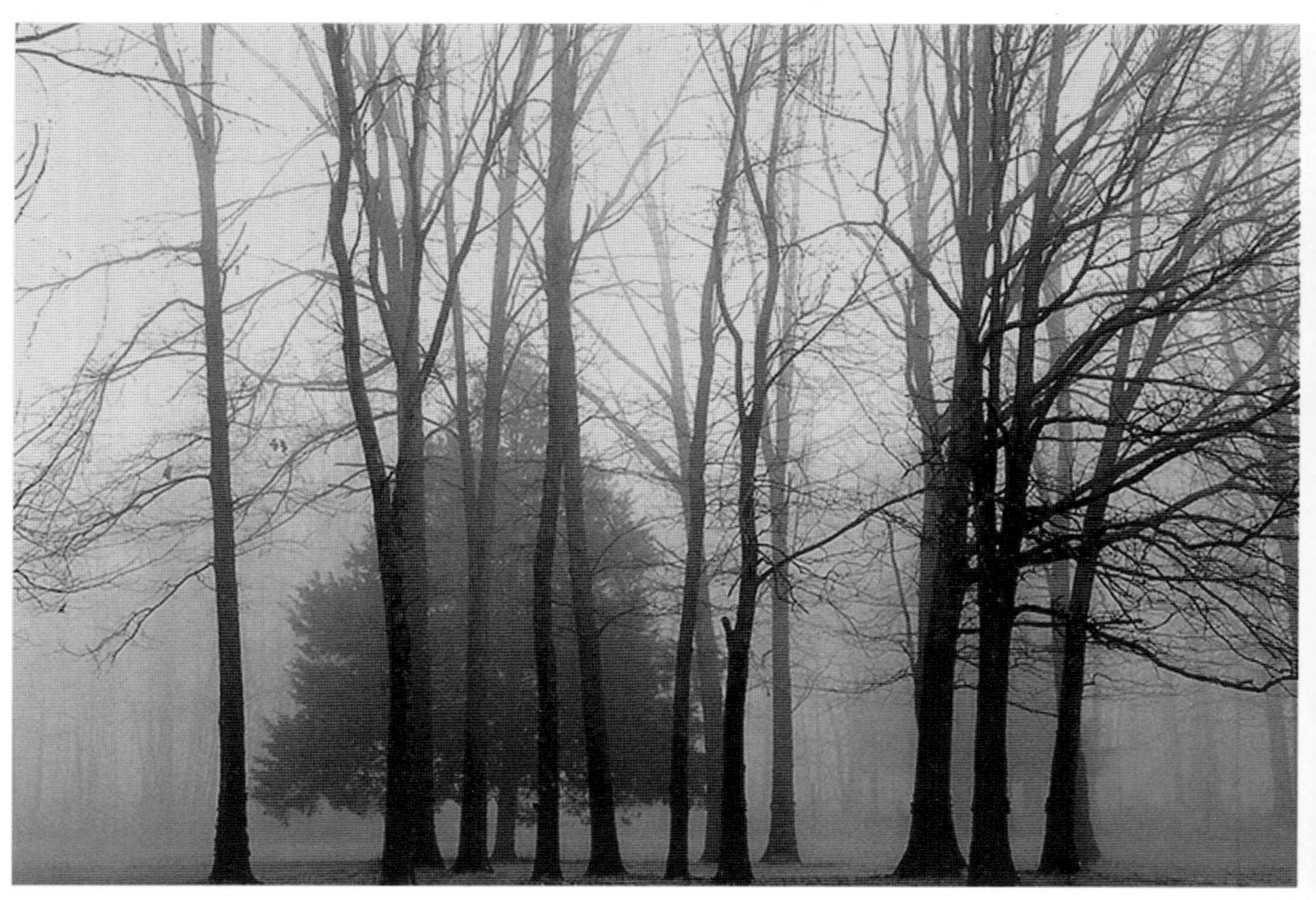

The Mists of Spring Greene County, MO

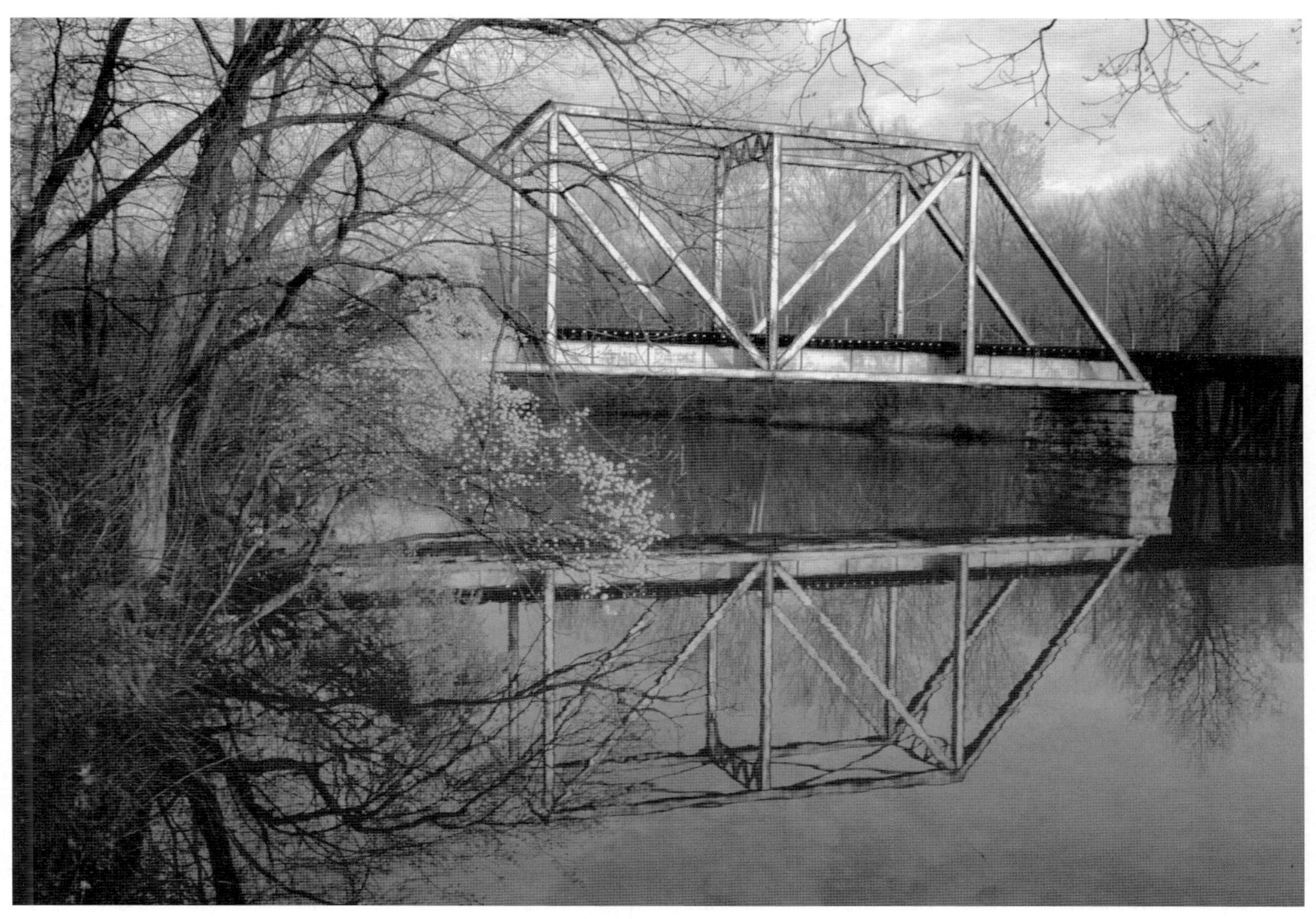

Old Train Bridge-Lake Springfield-Springfield, MO

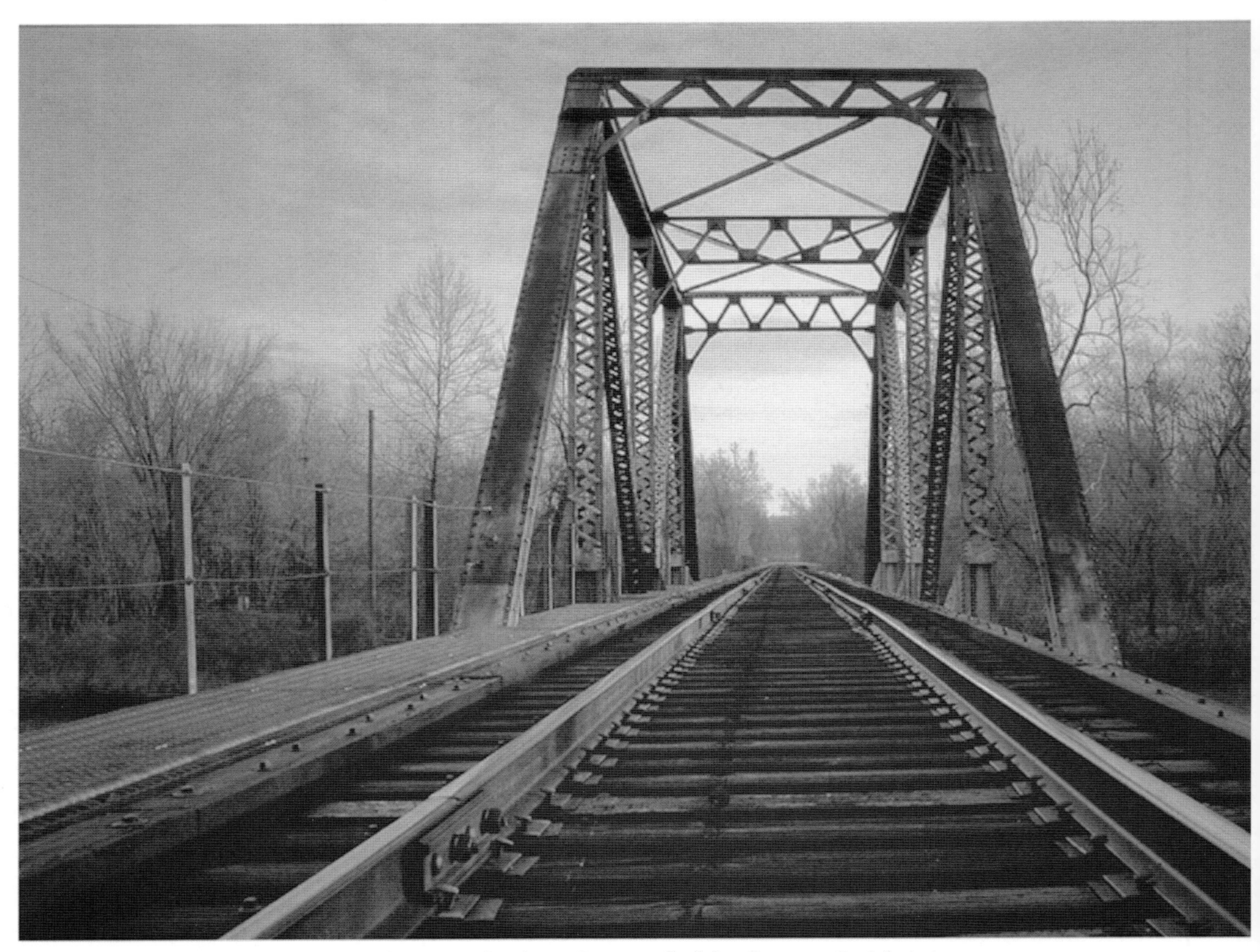

Old Train Bridge Second View-Lake Springfield-Springfield, Missouri

Sam's Throne at the bottom of the cliffs near Mt. Judea, Arkansas

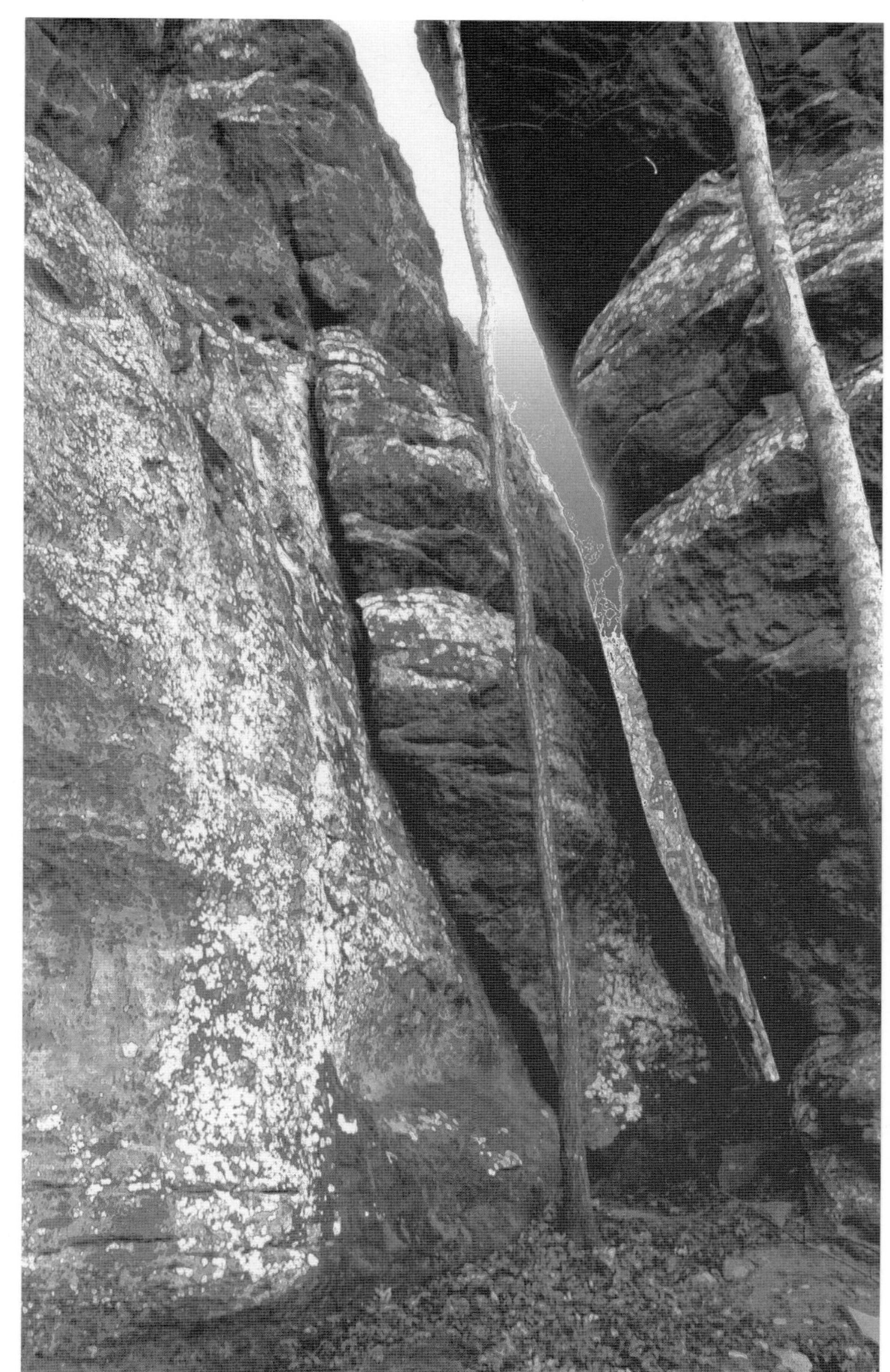

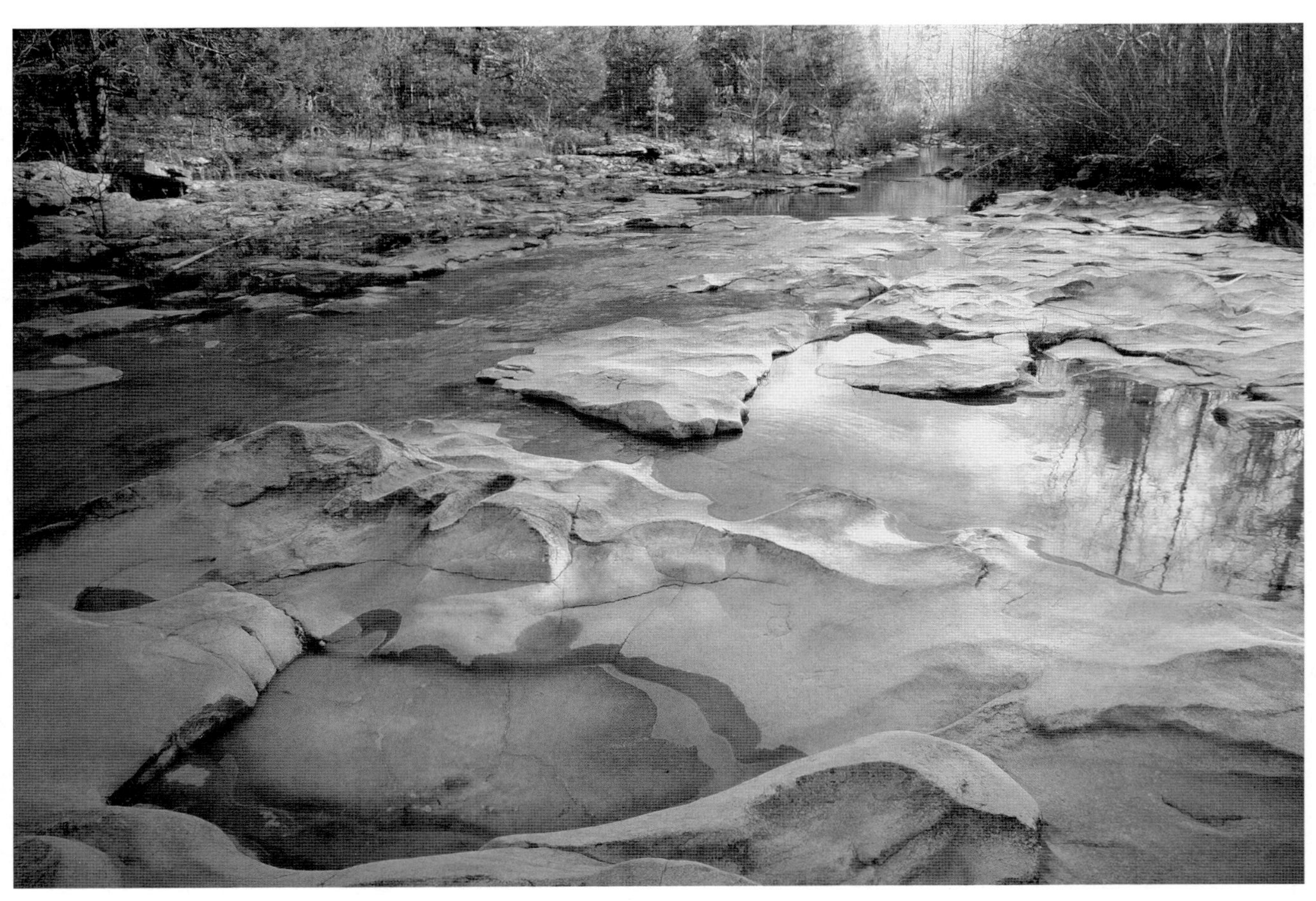

Falling Water Creek near Ben Hur, Arkansas

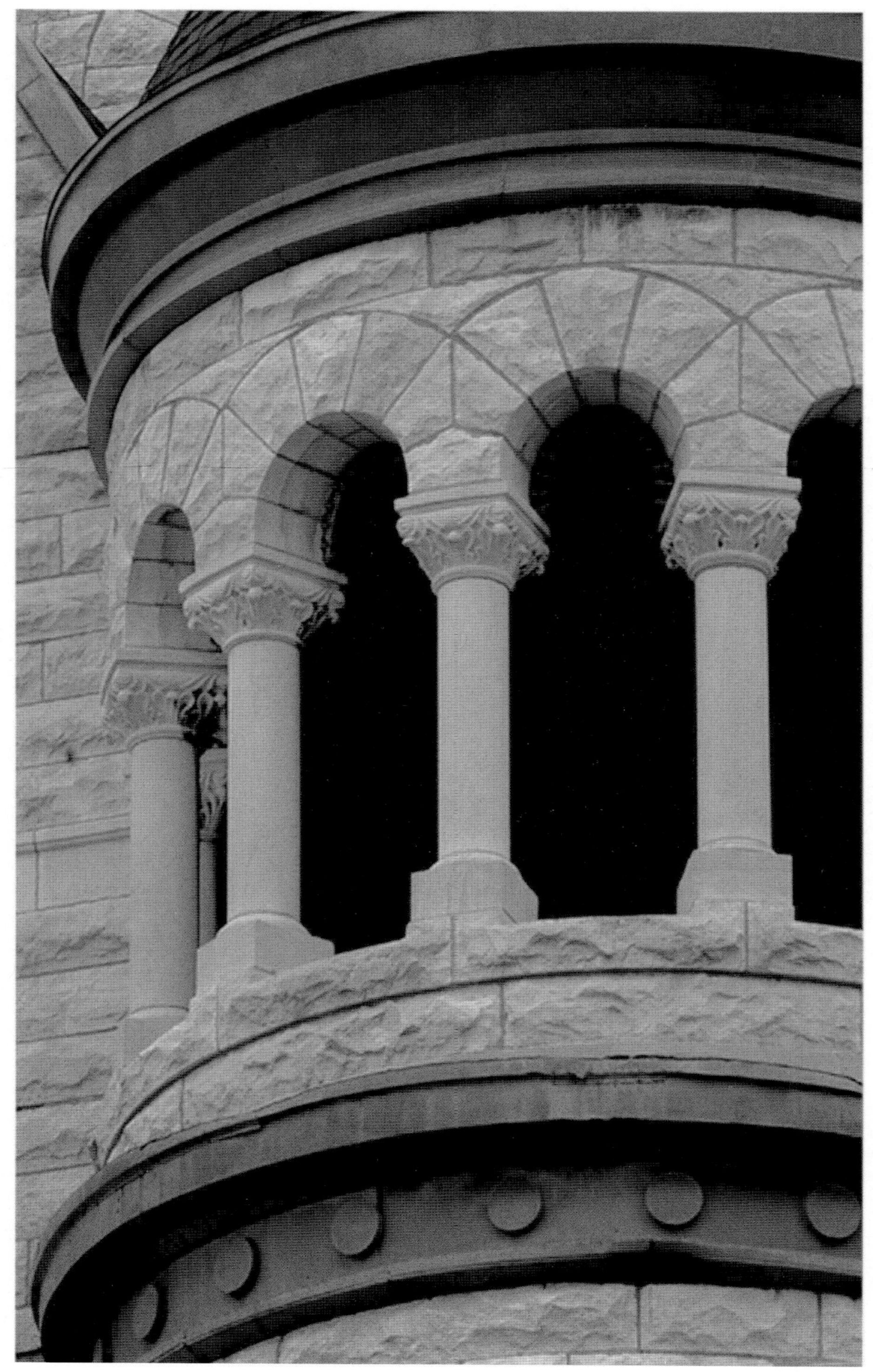

Jasper County
Courthouse
Carthage, Missouri

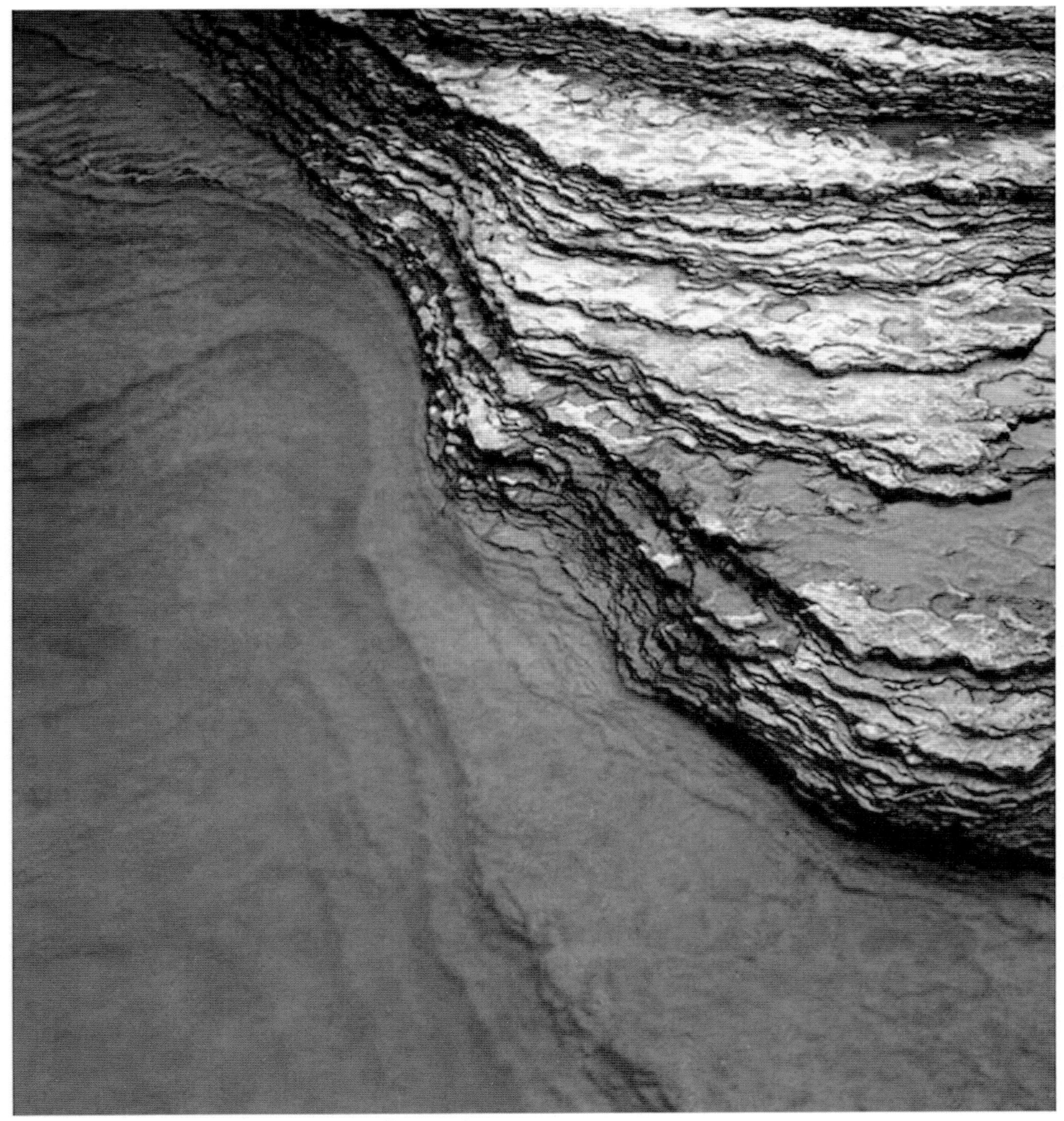

Six Finger Falls near Mossville, Arkansas

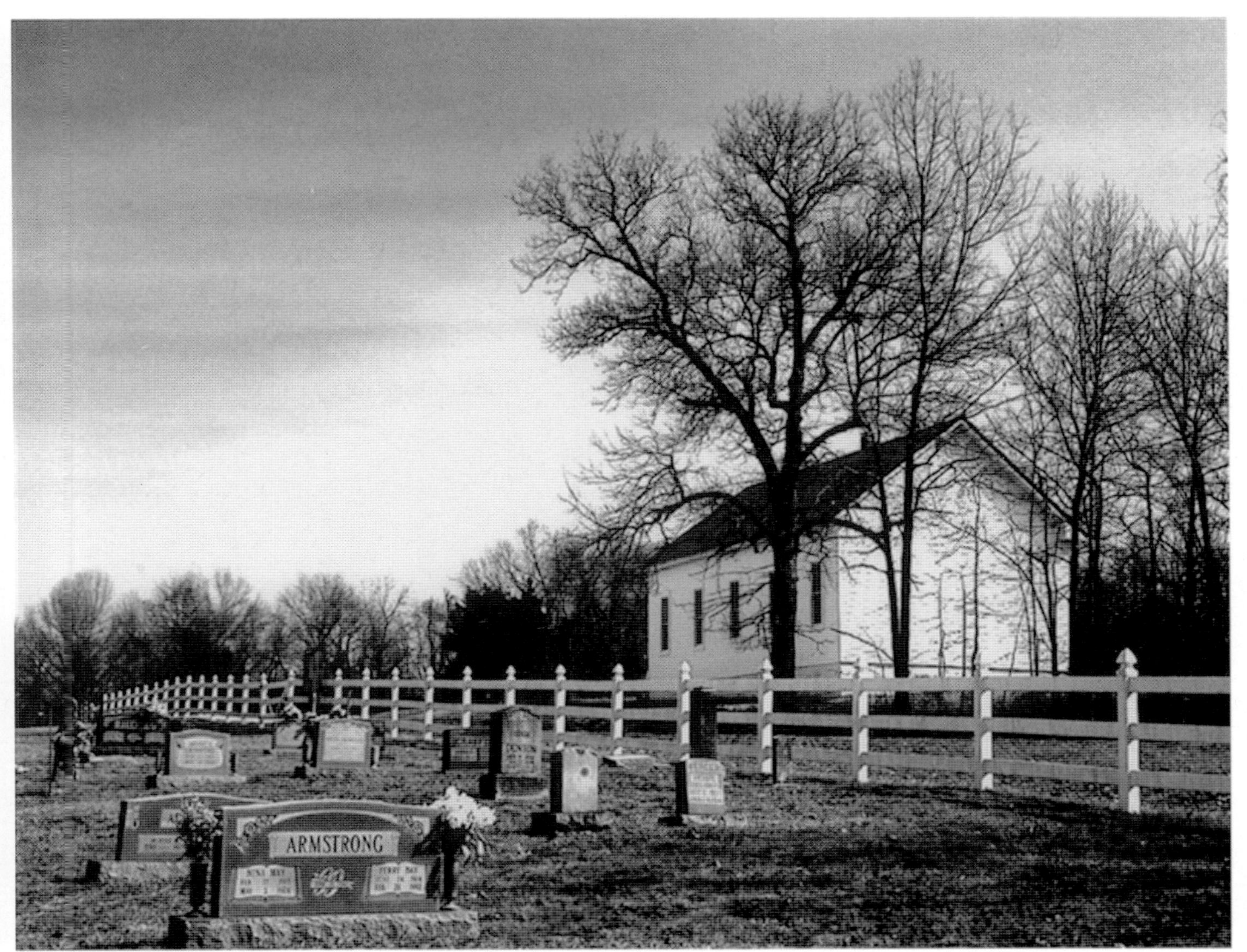

Union Church & Cemetery north of Cabool, Missouri

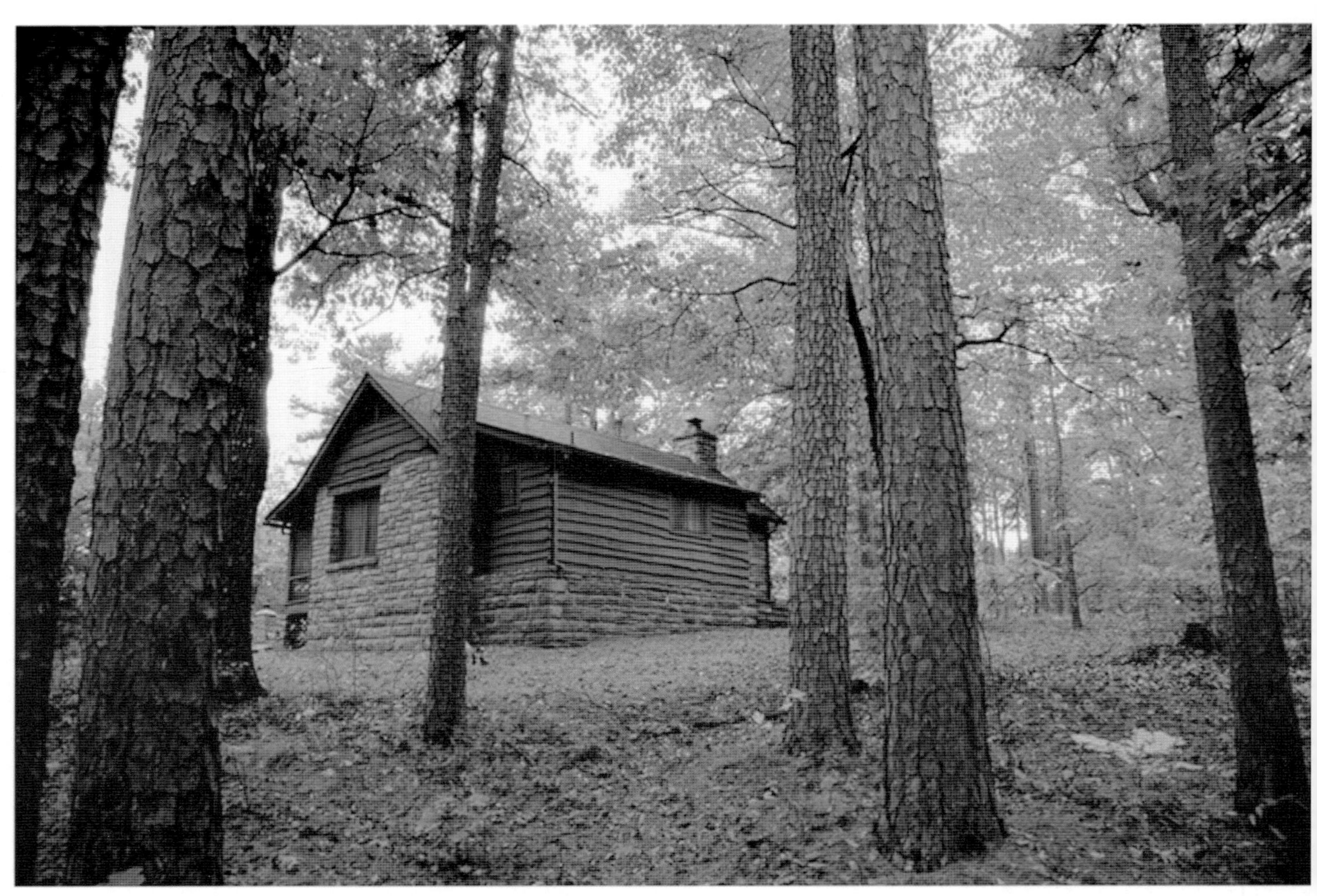

Cabin in the Pines in Buffalo Point State Park, Arkansas

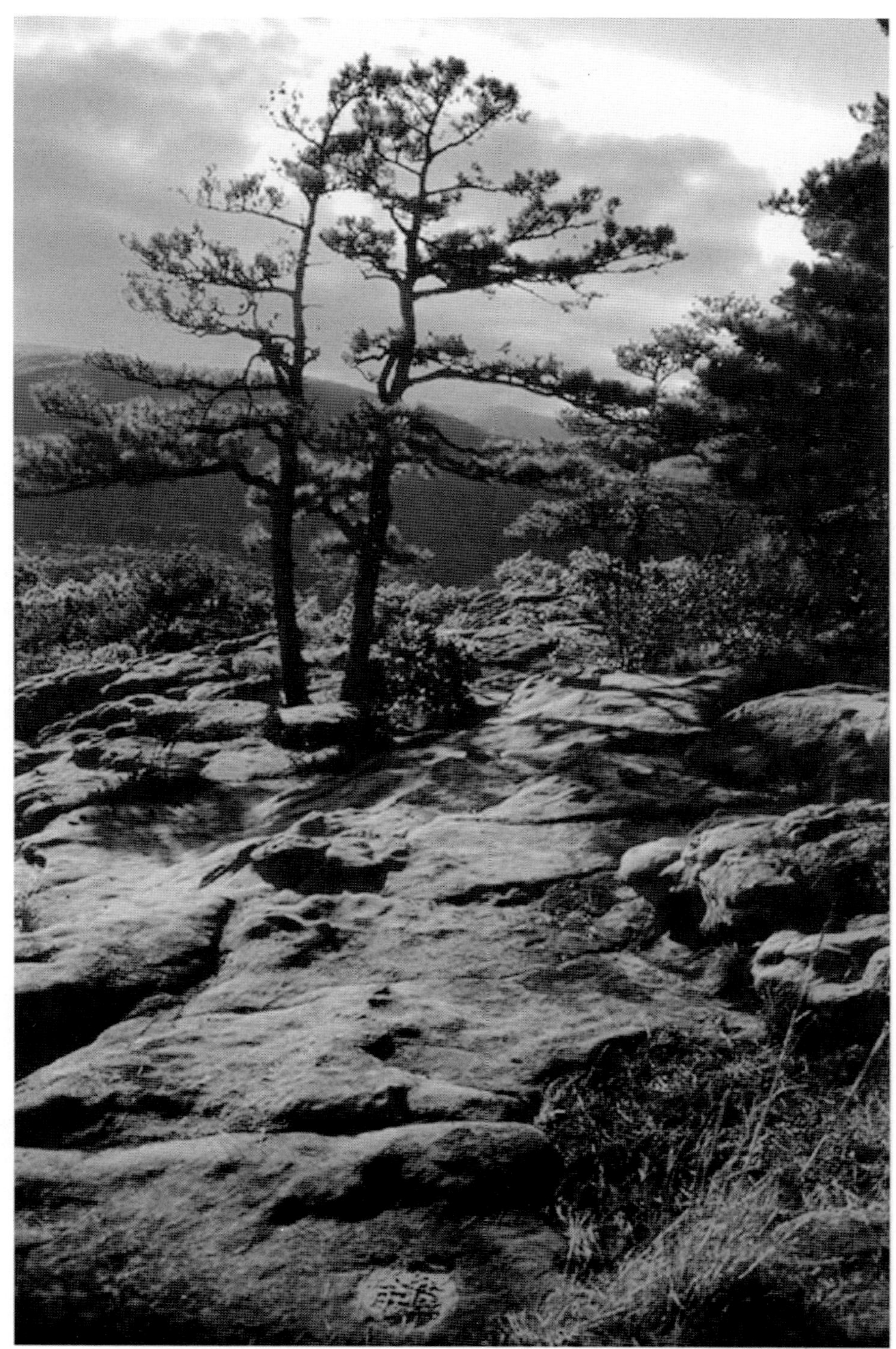

Stone Bound
Sam's Throne near
Mt. Judea, Arkansas

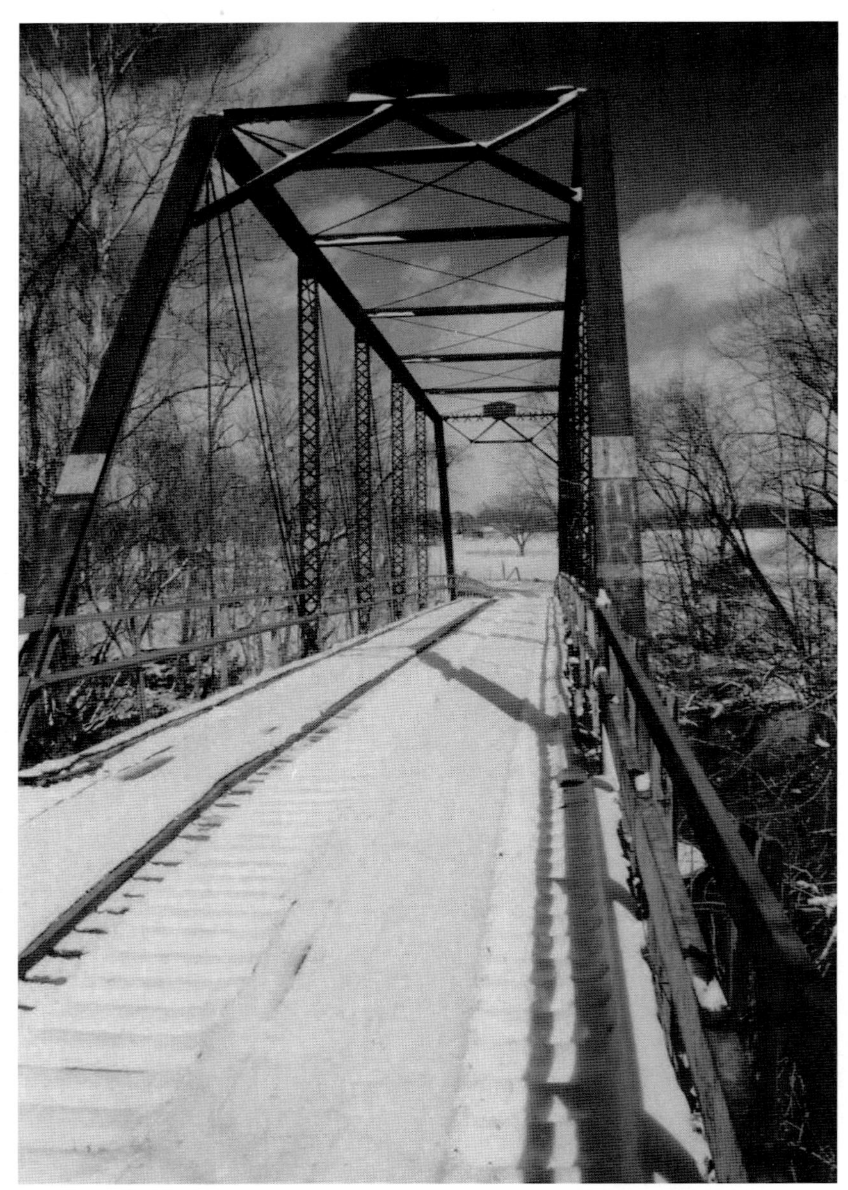

The Old Green Bridge over the Finley River
Ozark, Misouri

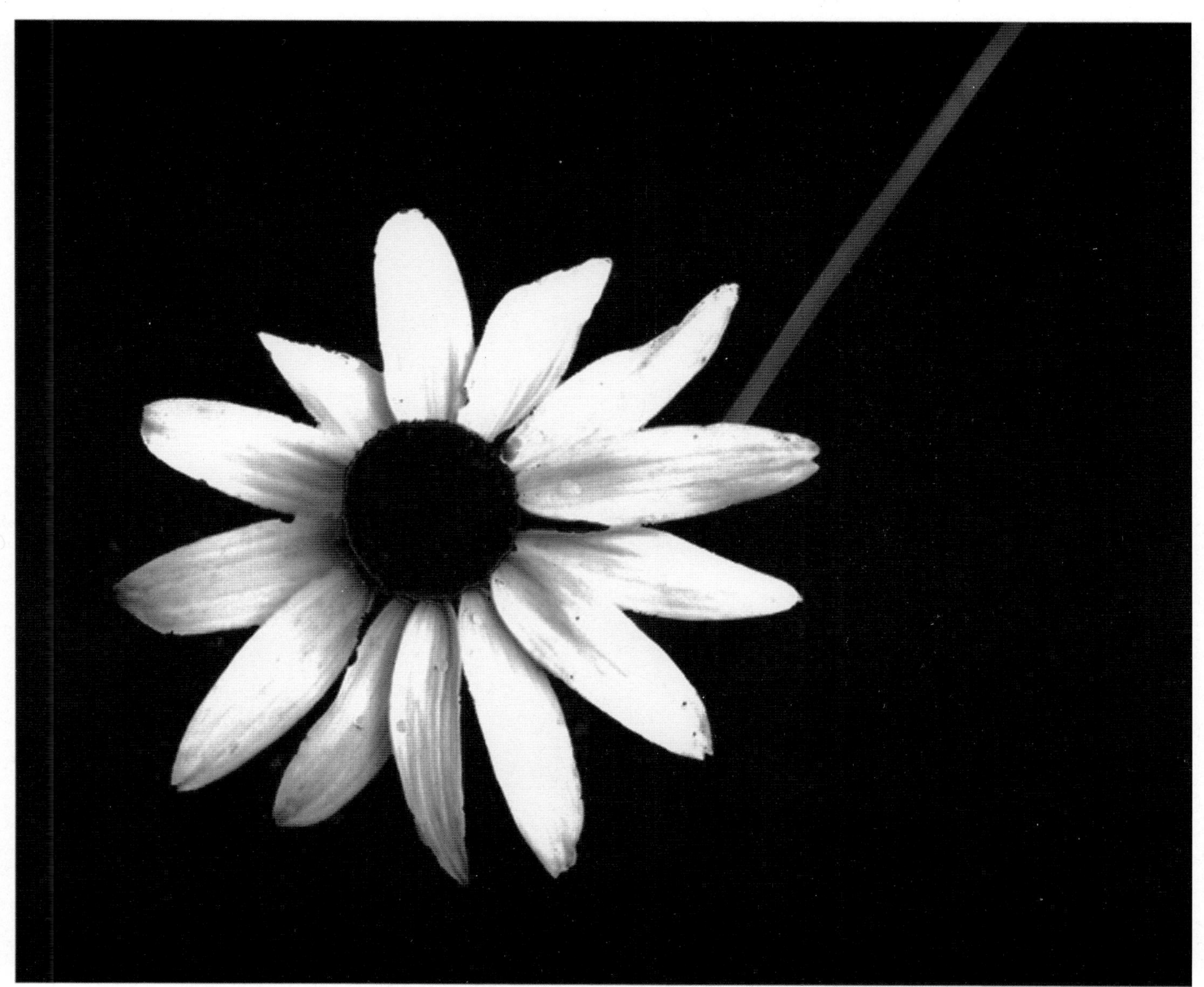

Black-eyed Susan

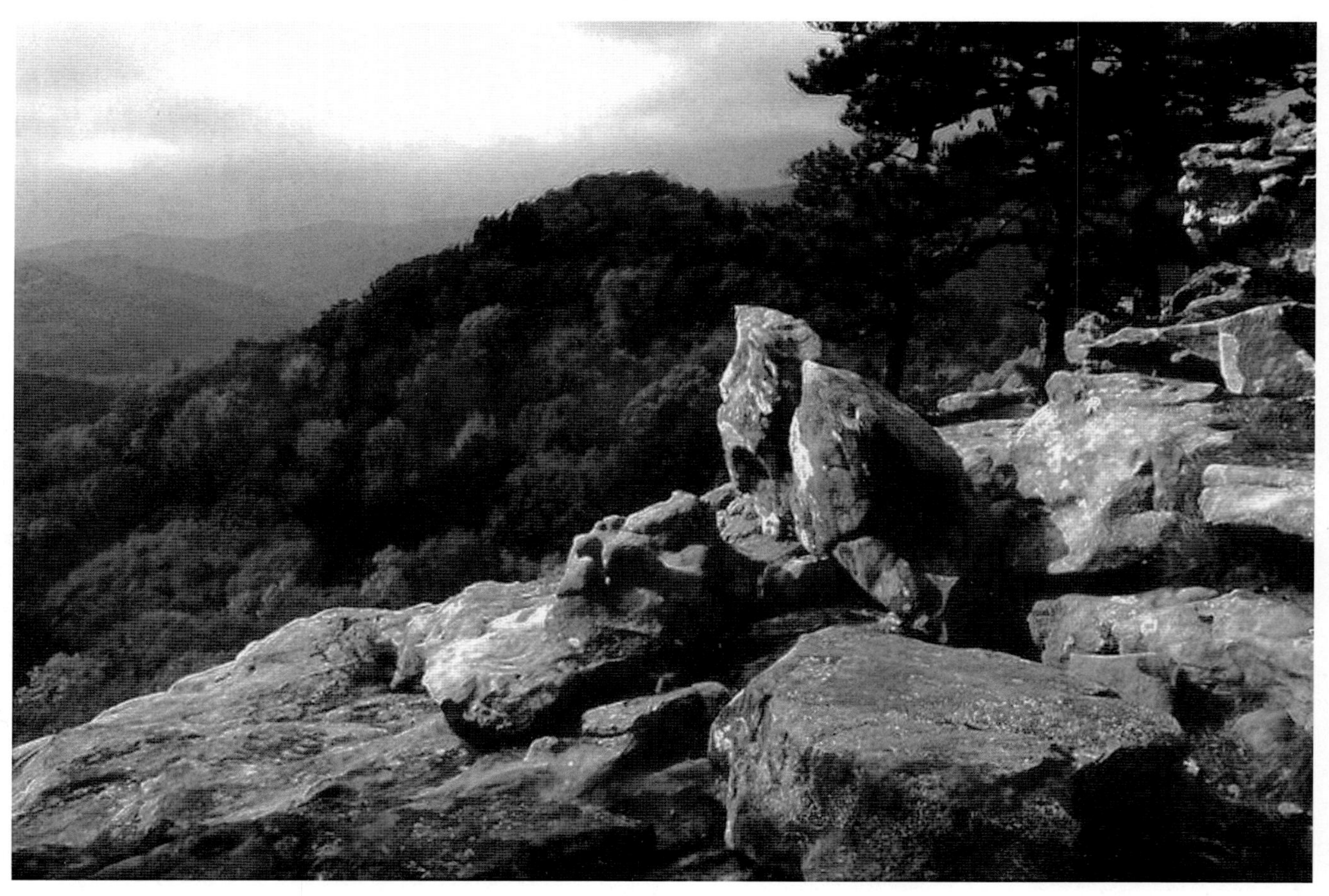

Sam's Throne- Mt. Judea, Arkansas

The name is derived from a possibly fictional character named Sam. Some say he was a deranged itinerate preacher who would deliver sermons from the tops of the cliffs.

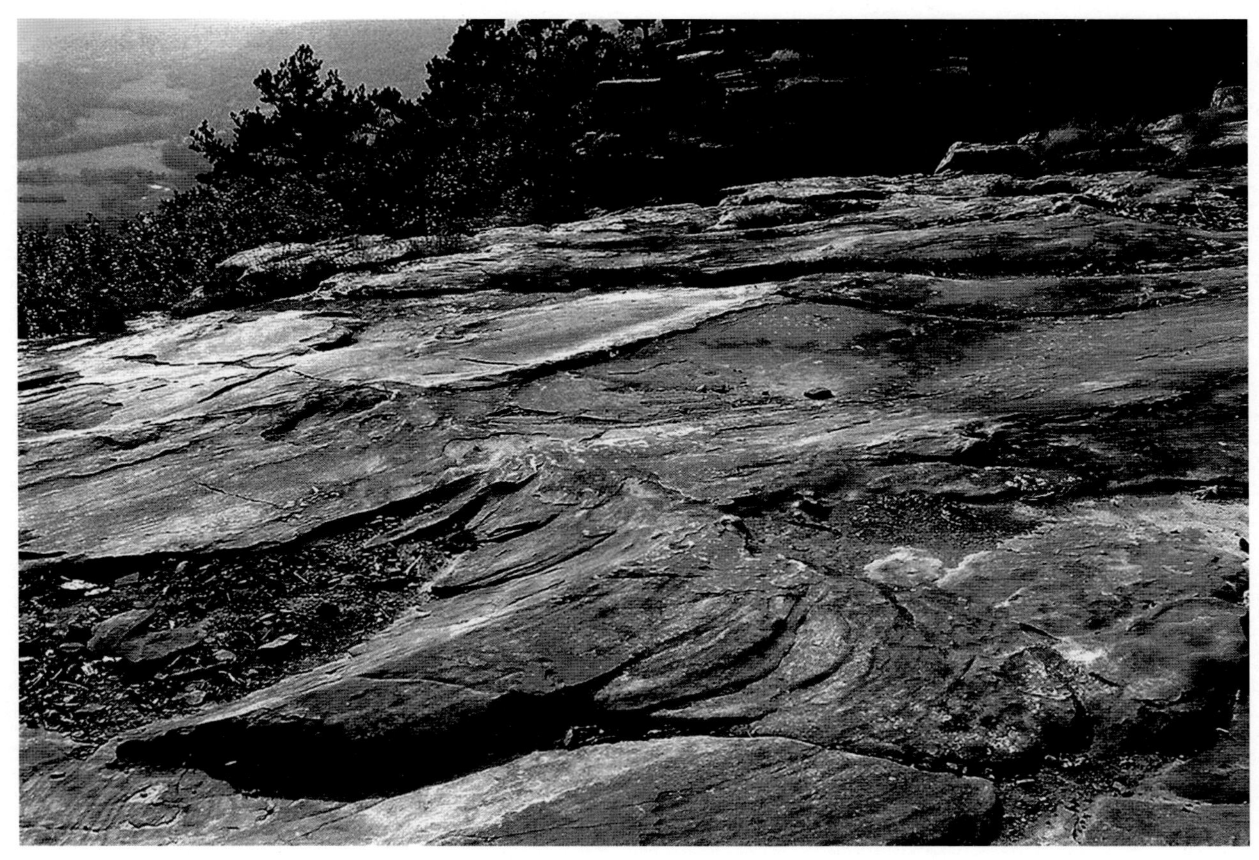

Timeswept

Sam's Throne-Mt. Judea, Arkansas

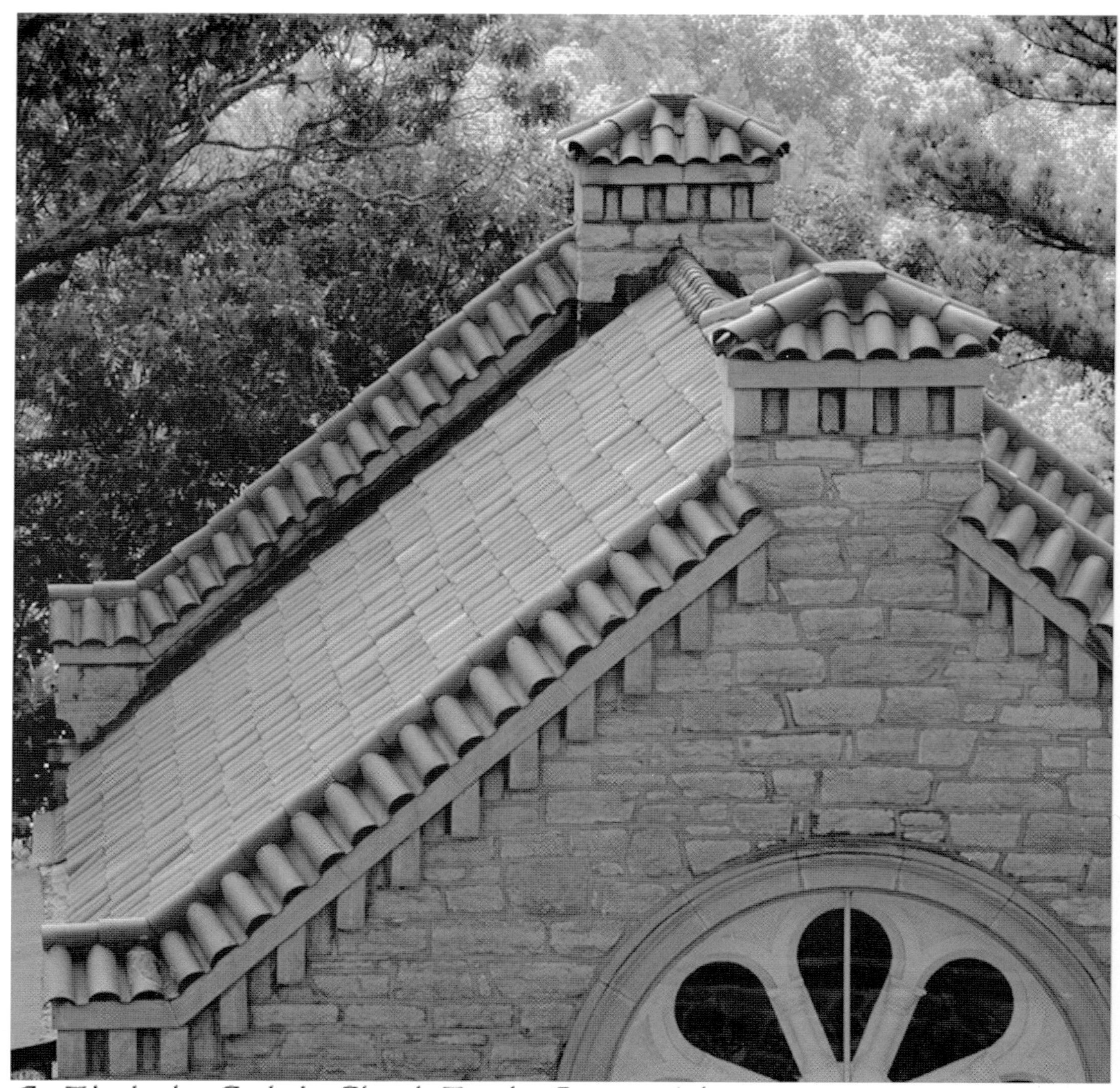

St. Elizabeth's Catholic Church-Eureka Springs, Arkansas

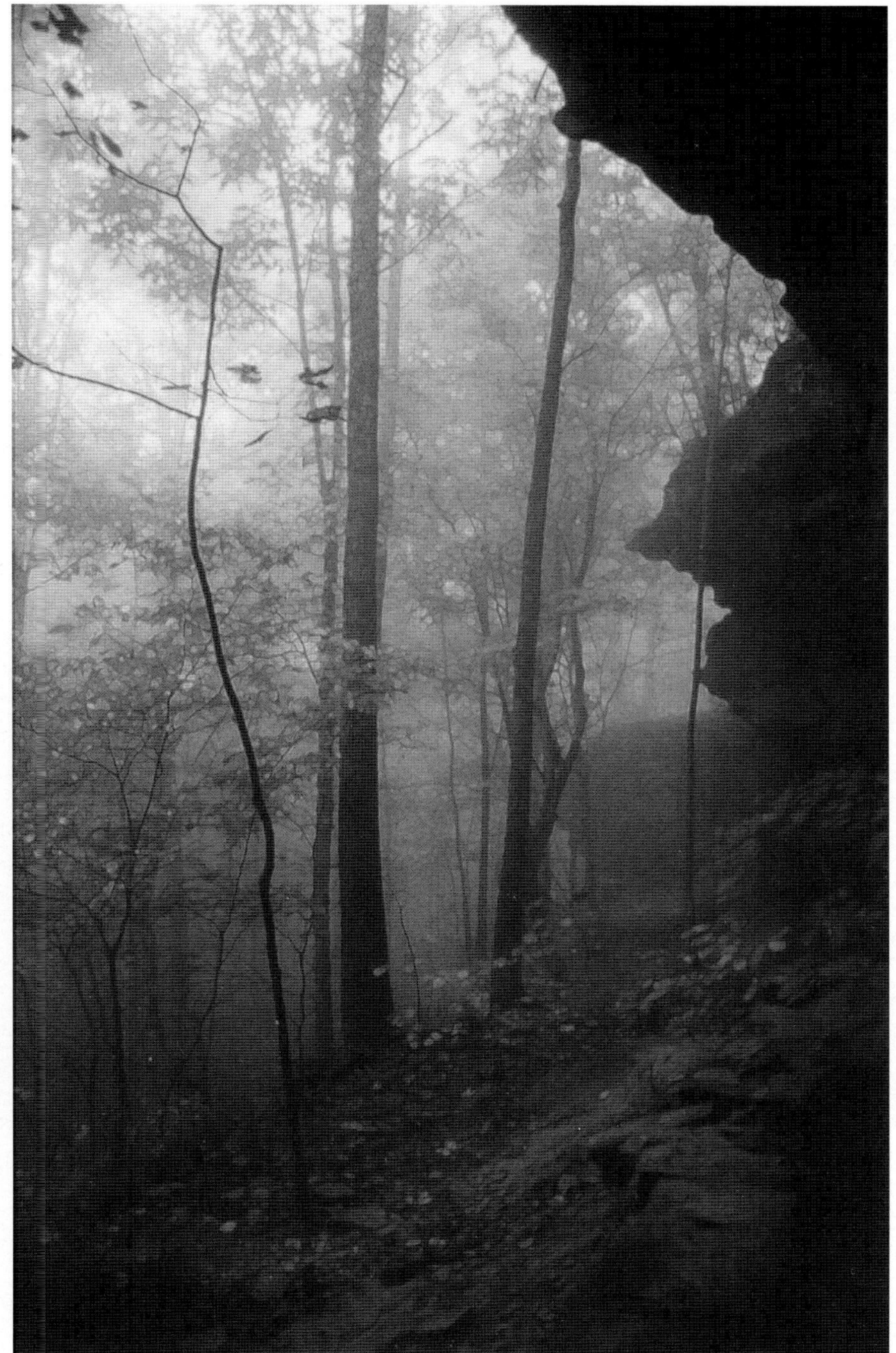

Boen Gulf-Upper Buffalo Wilderness Area-Arkansas

The Ghosts of October

Trees dimly gleaming
in the October mists like
half-remembered thoughts
of old men's pasts

Like skeletal ghosts
they gather to mourn
the draining of life
from limbs cold and bare

To speak of the past
and dream of the spring
by the rattle of digits
like arthritic hands

Turned fragile and brittle
by the deepening cold
and the moaning wind
from the valleys below

Carl James

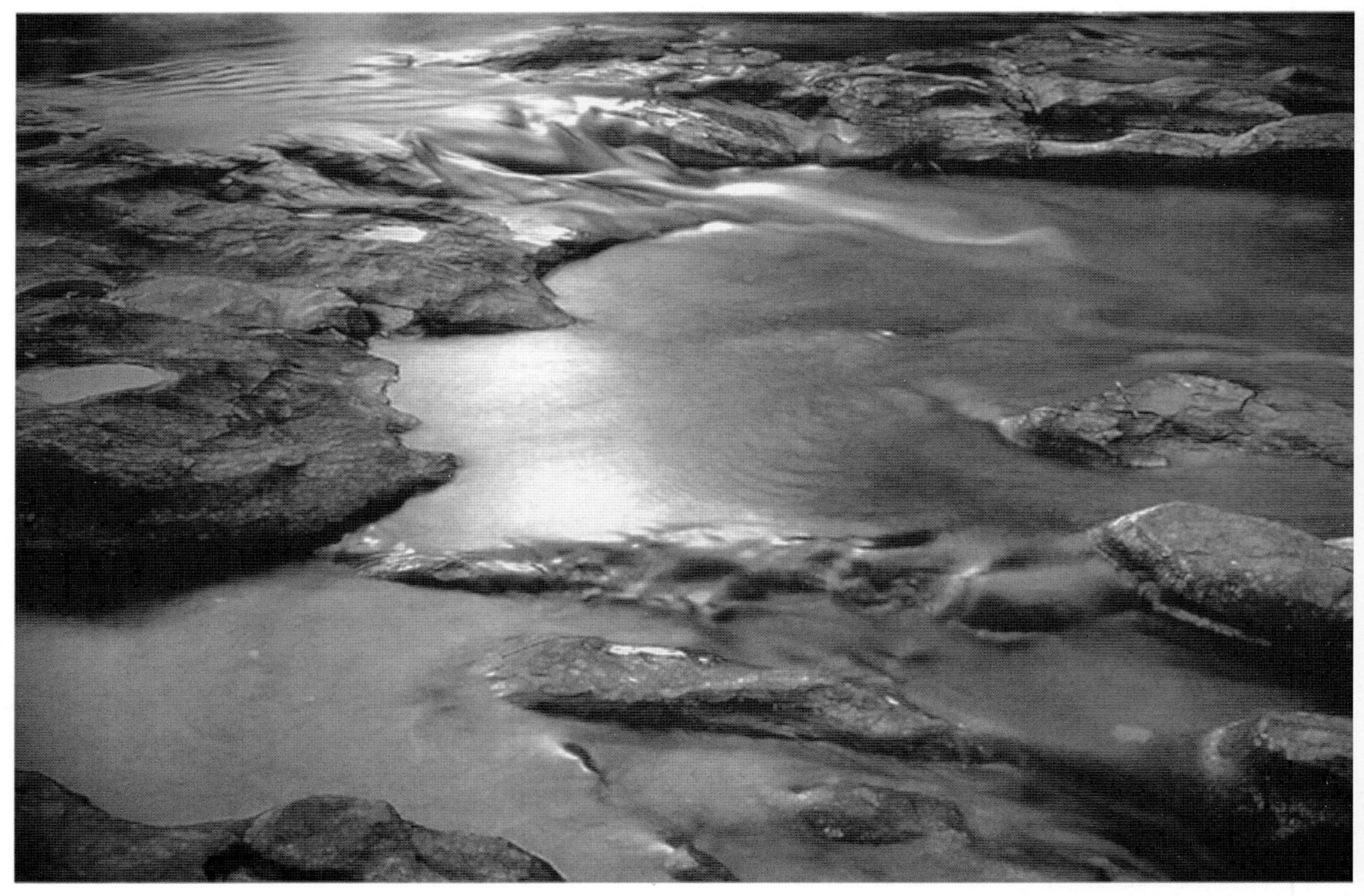

Quicksilver — Finley River Falls near Diggins, Missouri

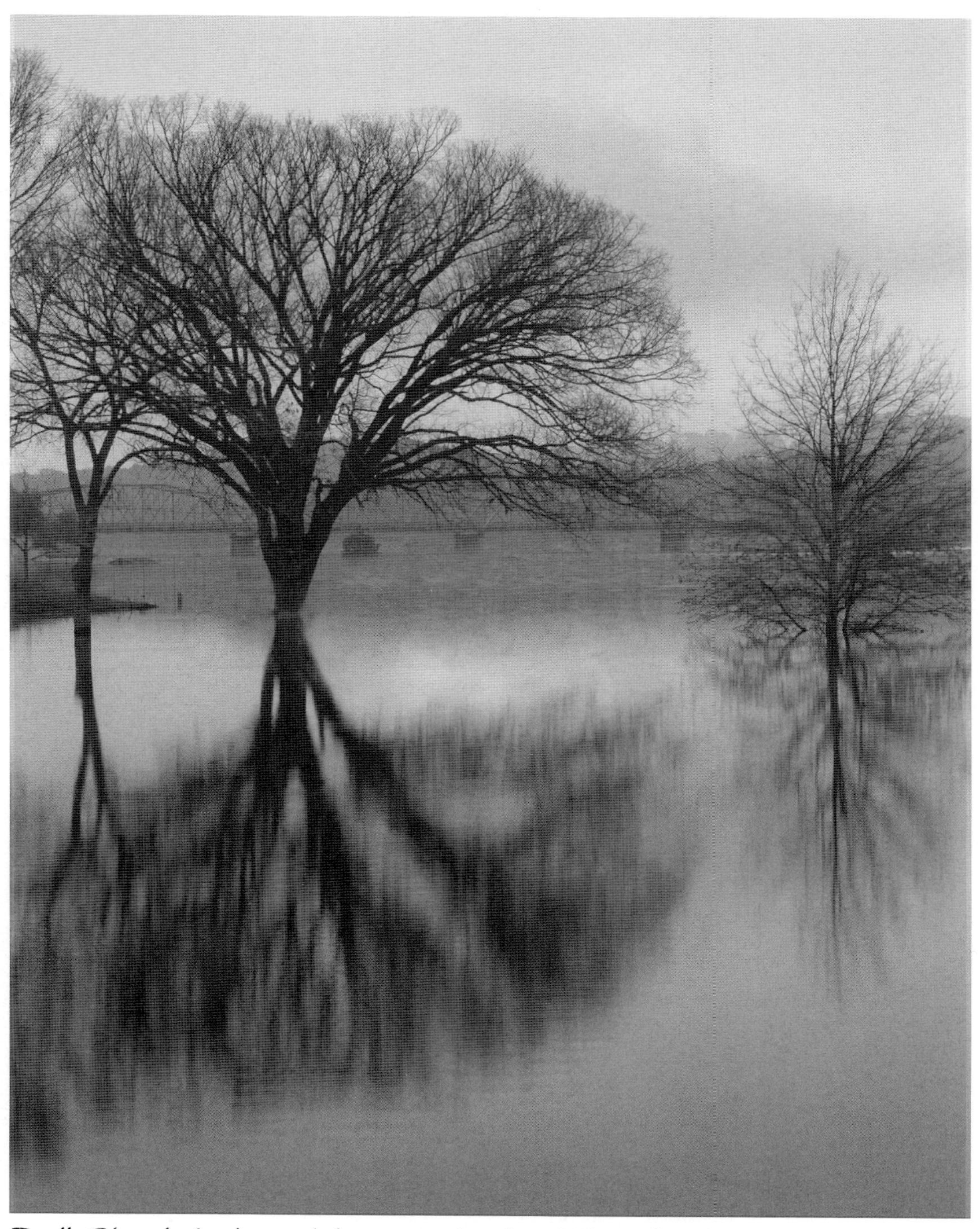

Bull Shoals Lake at Hwy. 160 bridge-Theodosia, Missouri

Falling Water Creek
Ben Hur, Arkansas

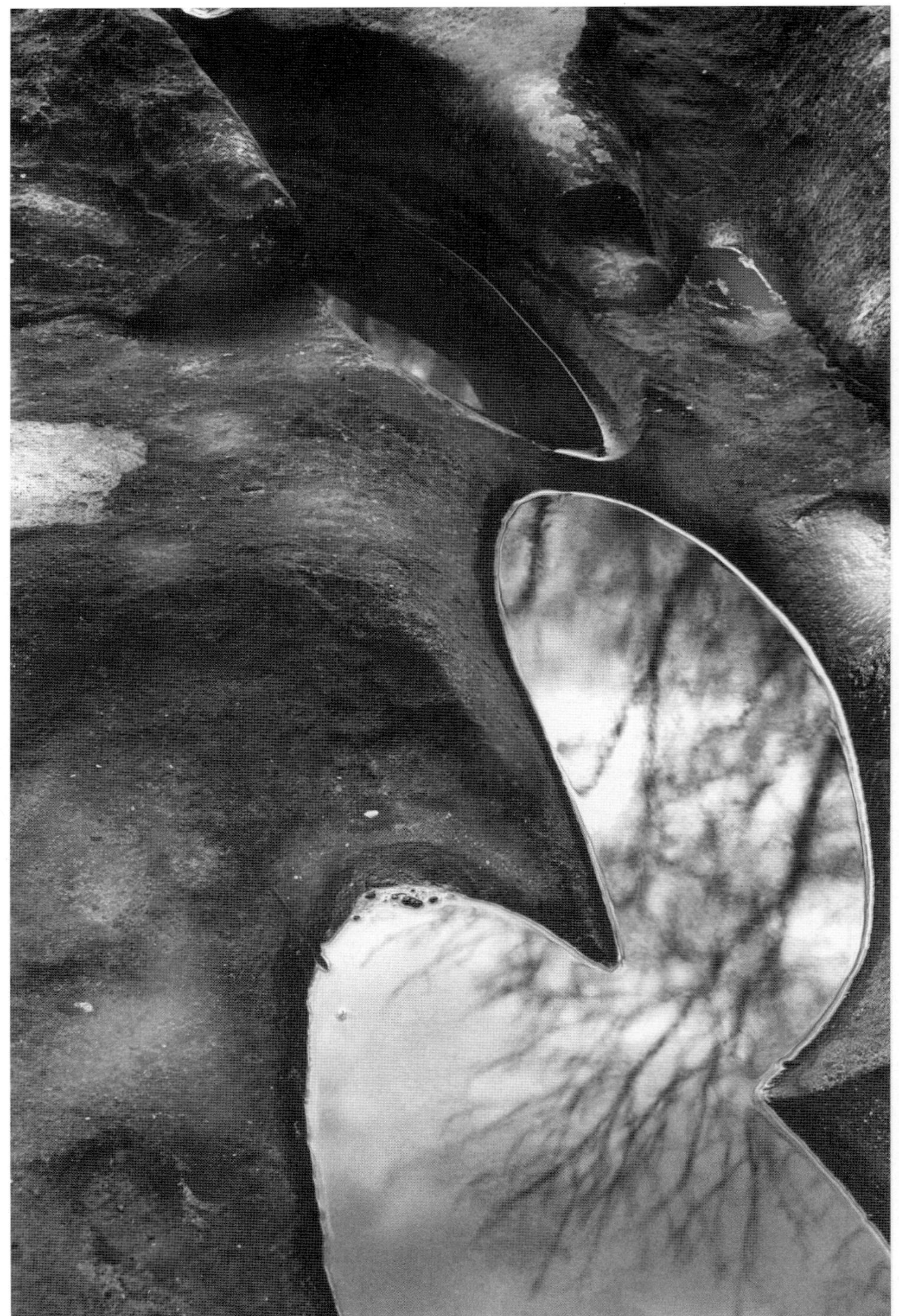

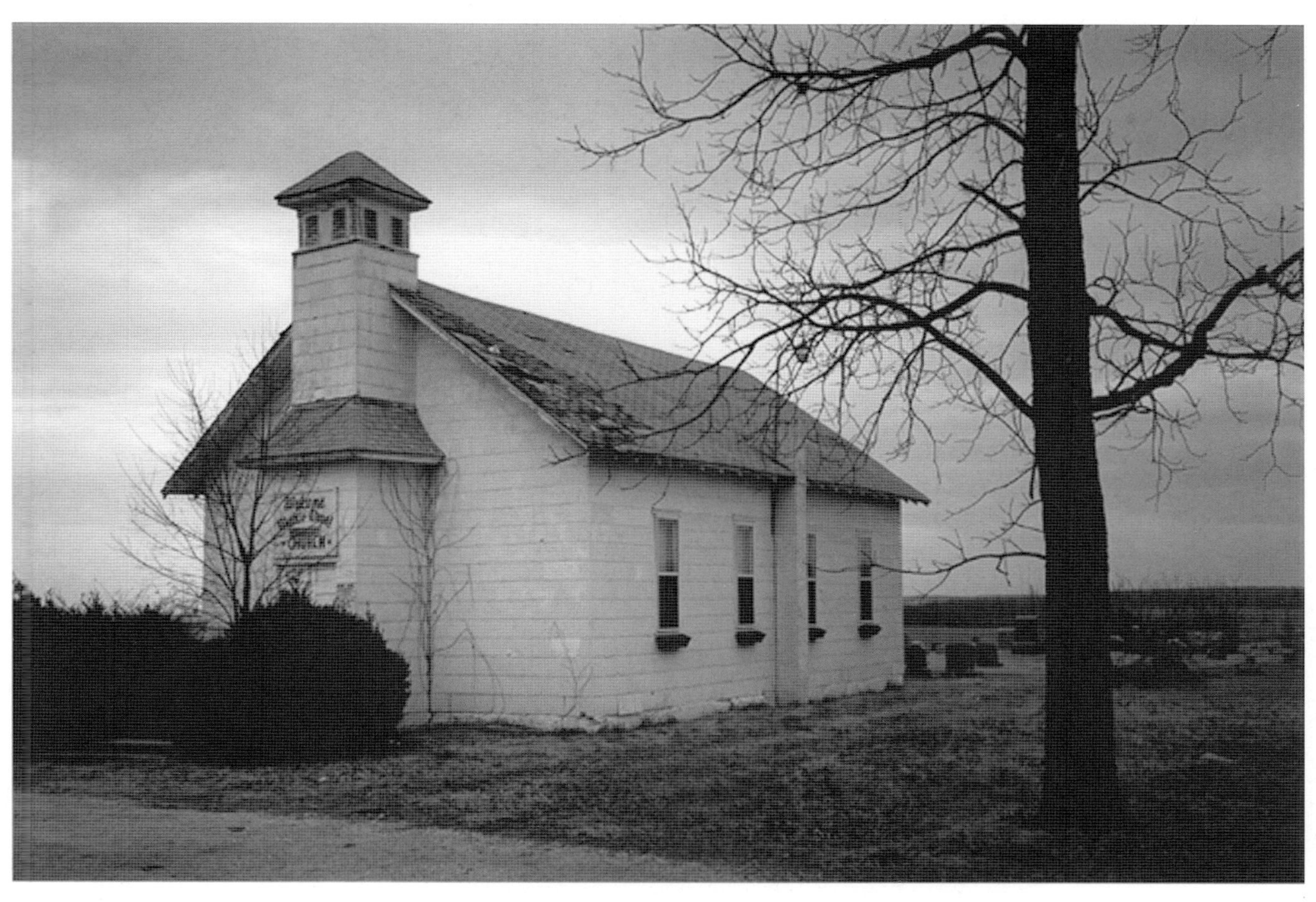

Muncie Chapel Missionary Church & Cemetery near Wheaton, Missouri

Farm Road #96 Greene County, MO

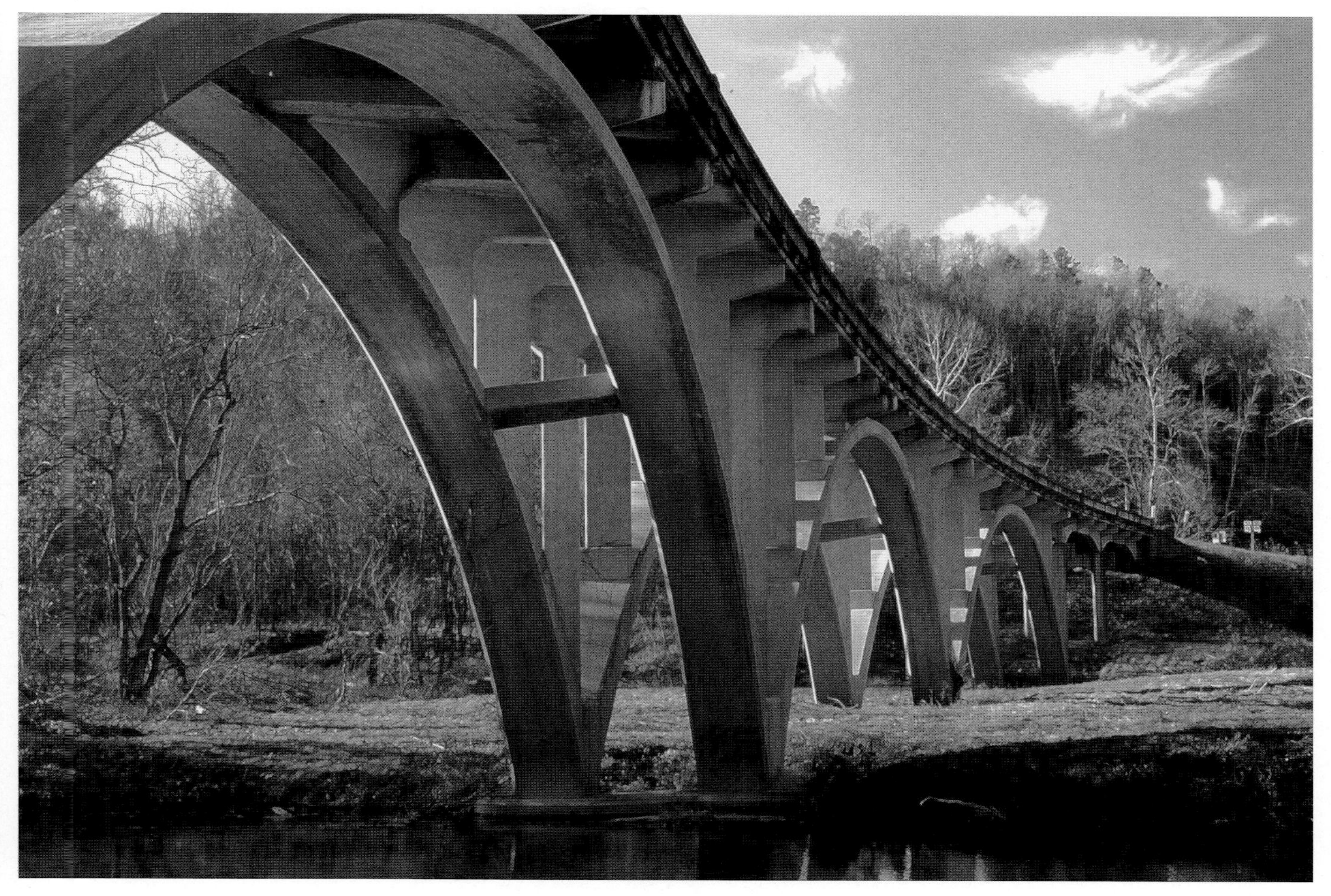

Twin Bridges on Missouri Hwy. #14 spanning the North Fork of the White River

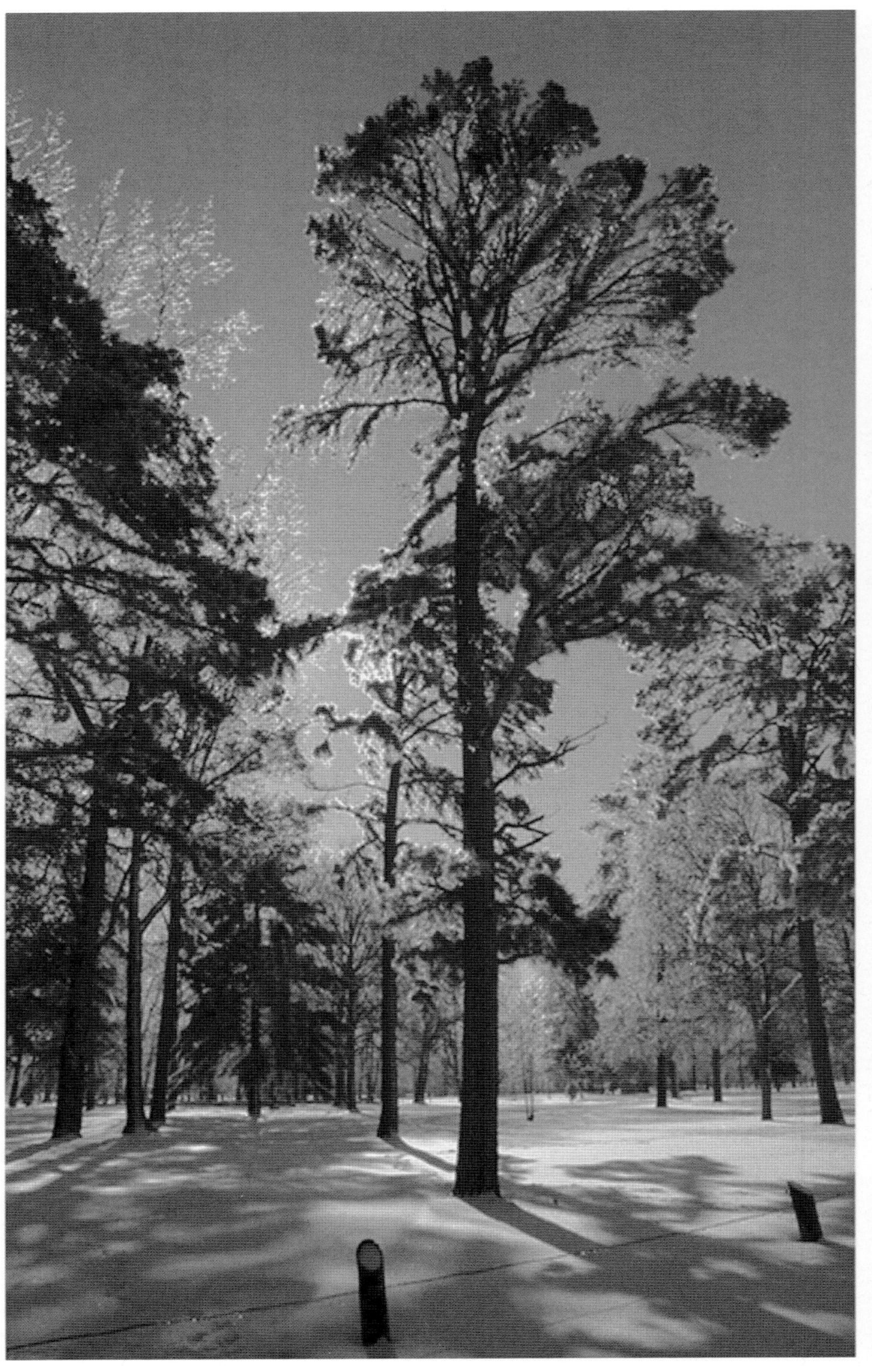

Phelps Grove Park Pines
Springfield, Missouri

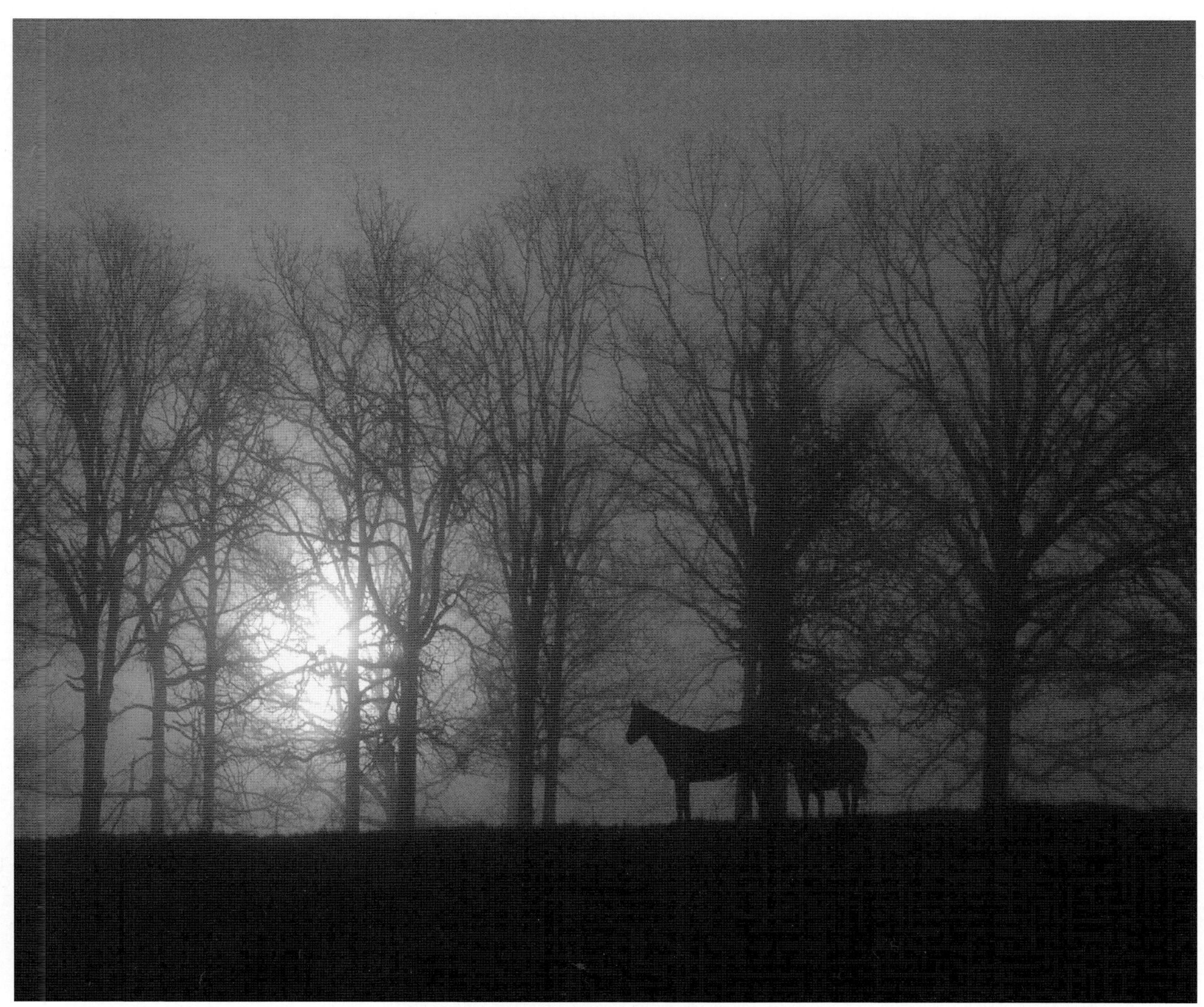

Along Farm Road #192, Greene County, MO

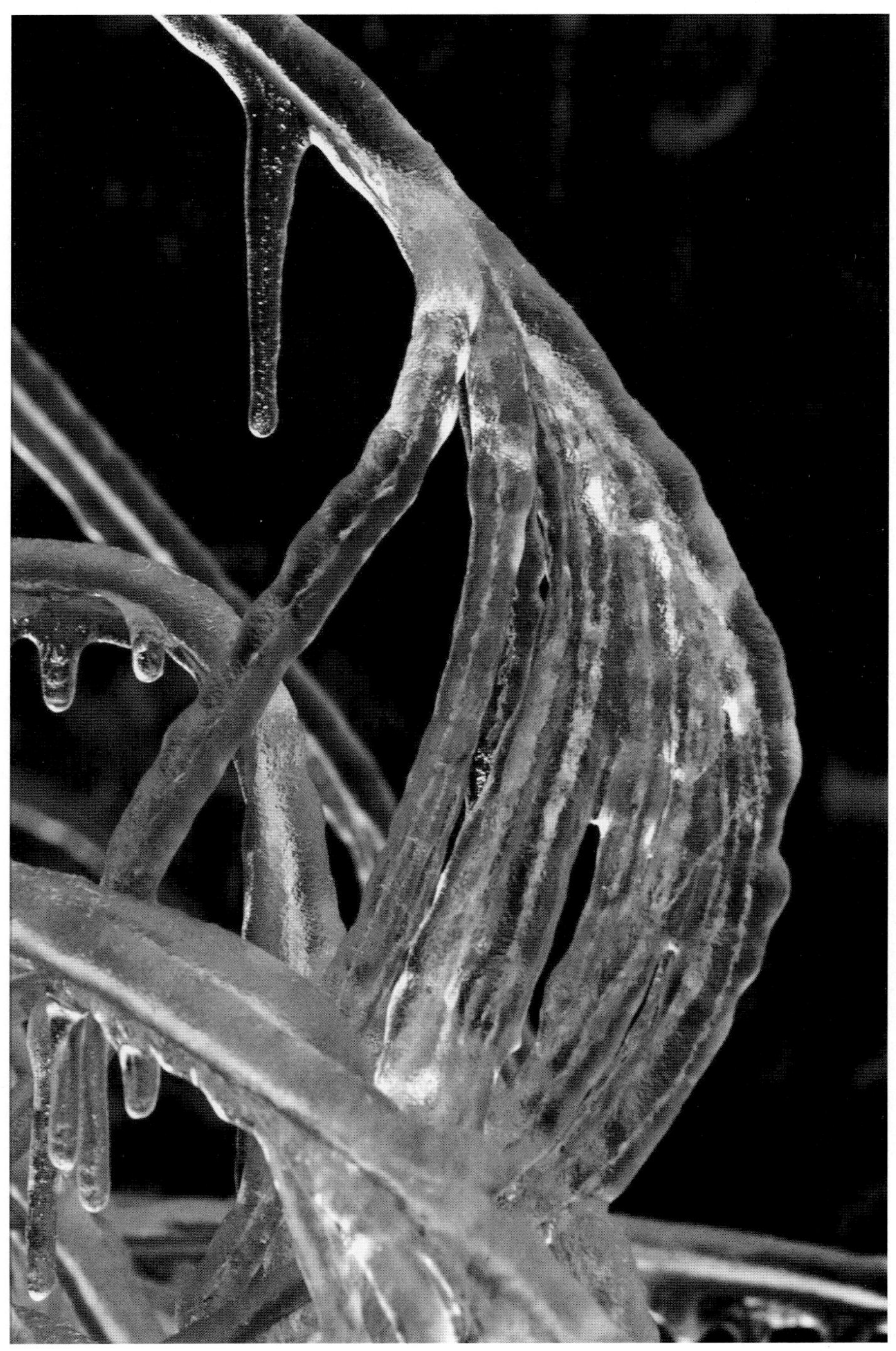

Behold the beauty in all nature's events even though its icy grip may lay waste to its own creations

Carl James

No structures on earth evoke more pride, emotions, human ingenuity and symbolism than bridges. Our best creative effort and innovation is focused on these structures. They represent connection to our neighbors and the world and reflect the pride and determination of a civilization. They are sculpture in its purist form.

Carl James

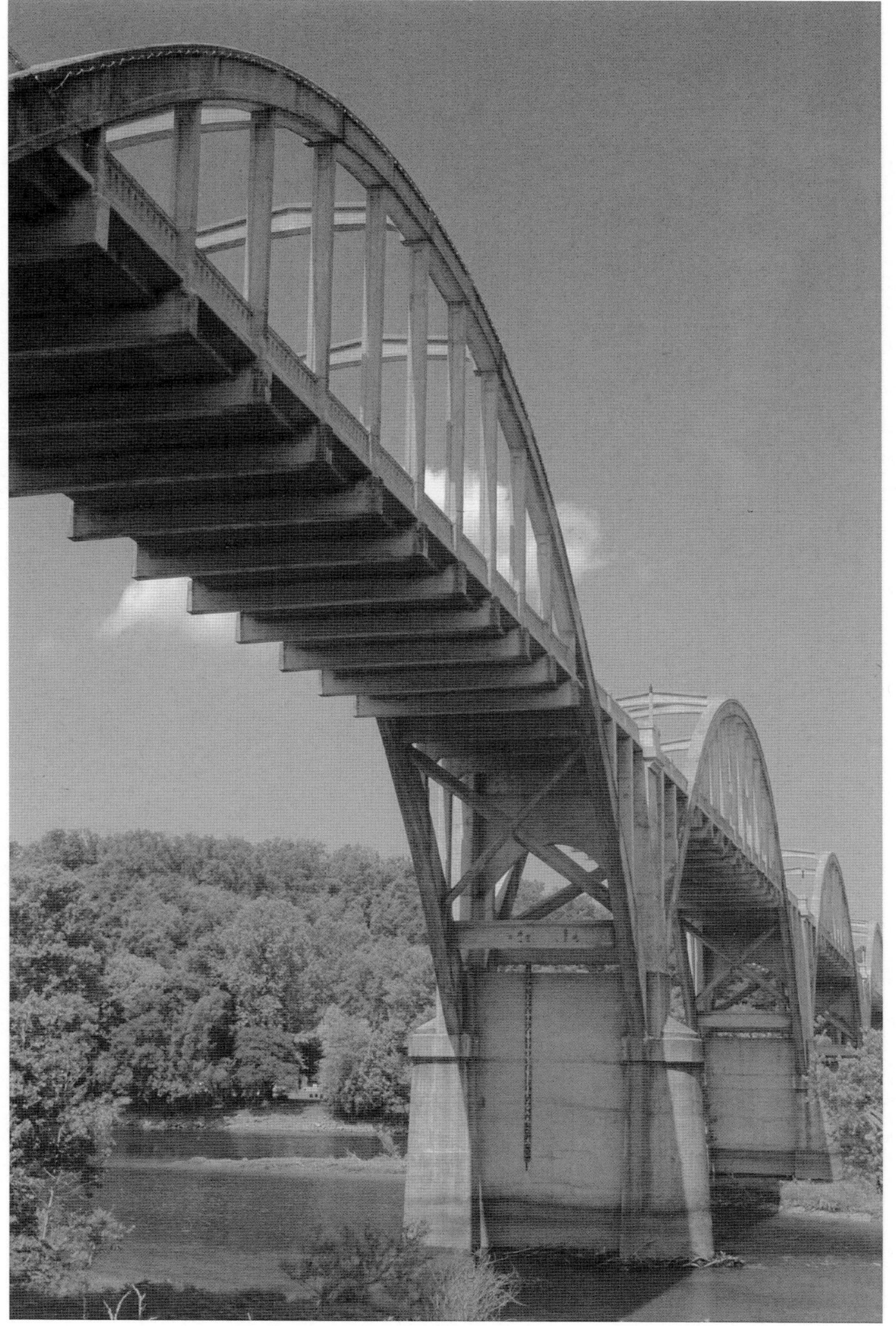

Hwy. 62B bridge across the White River near Cotter, AR

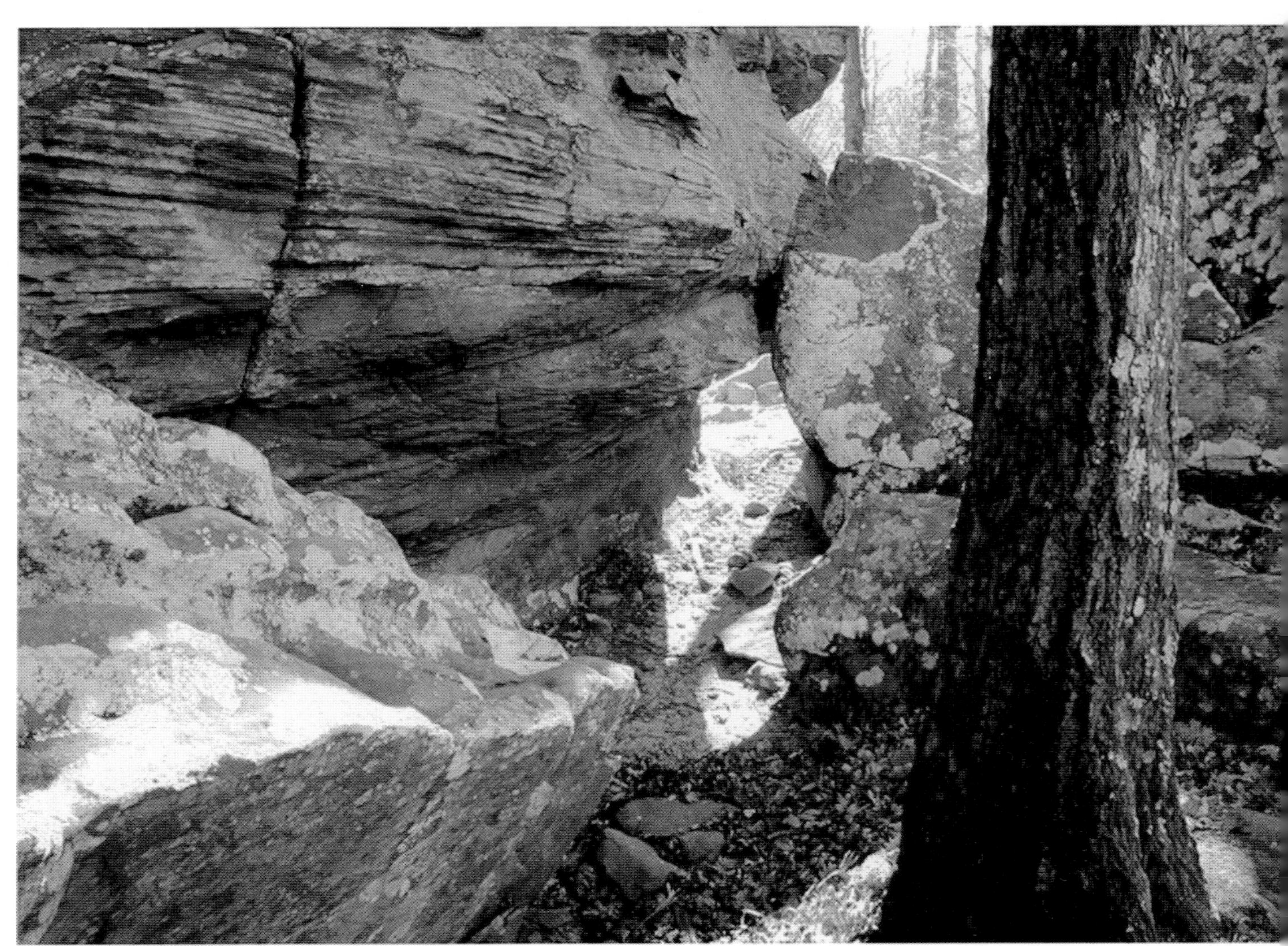

Sam's Throne-Mt. Judea, Arkansas

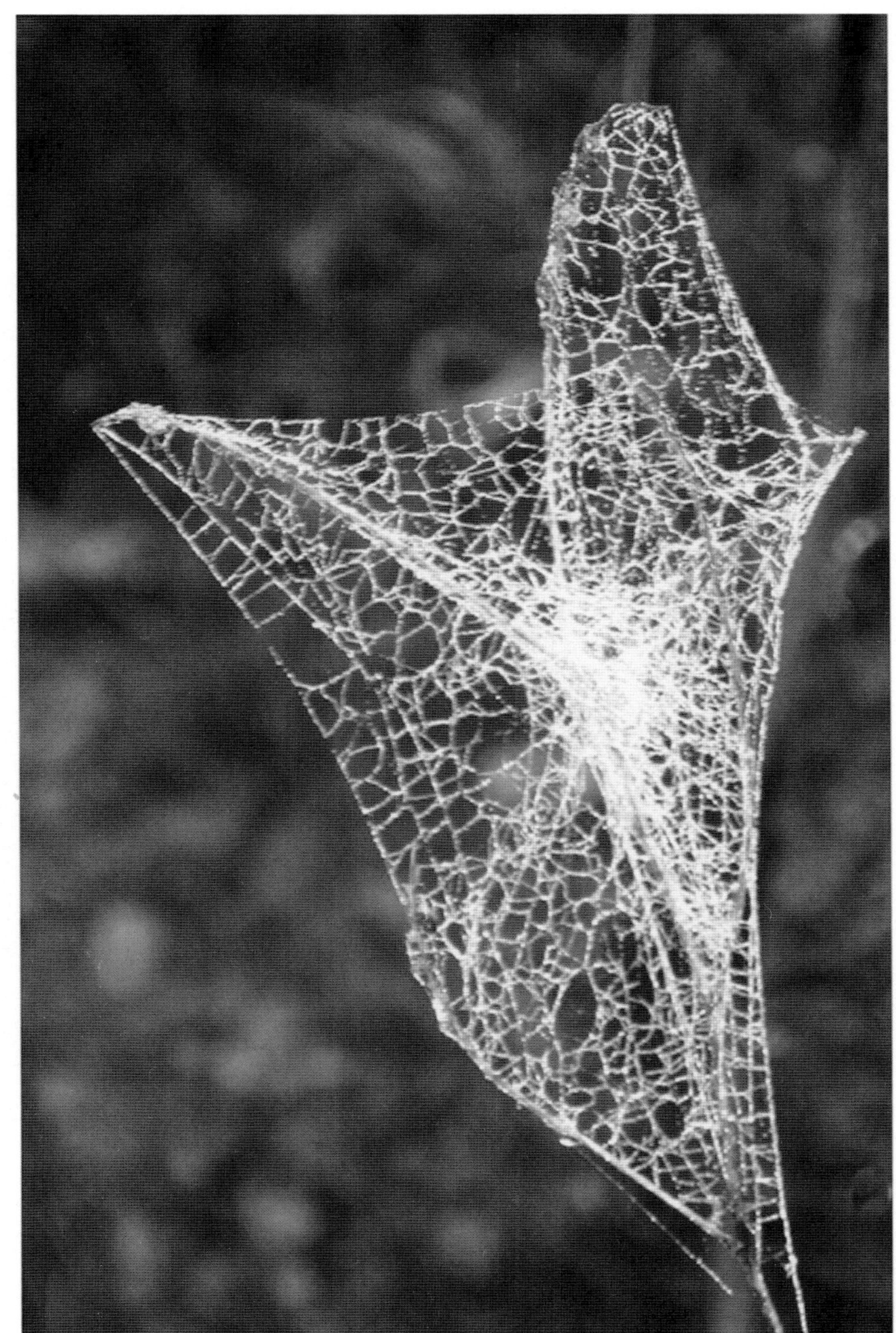

Early Morning
Webs-Ozark
County, Missouri

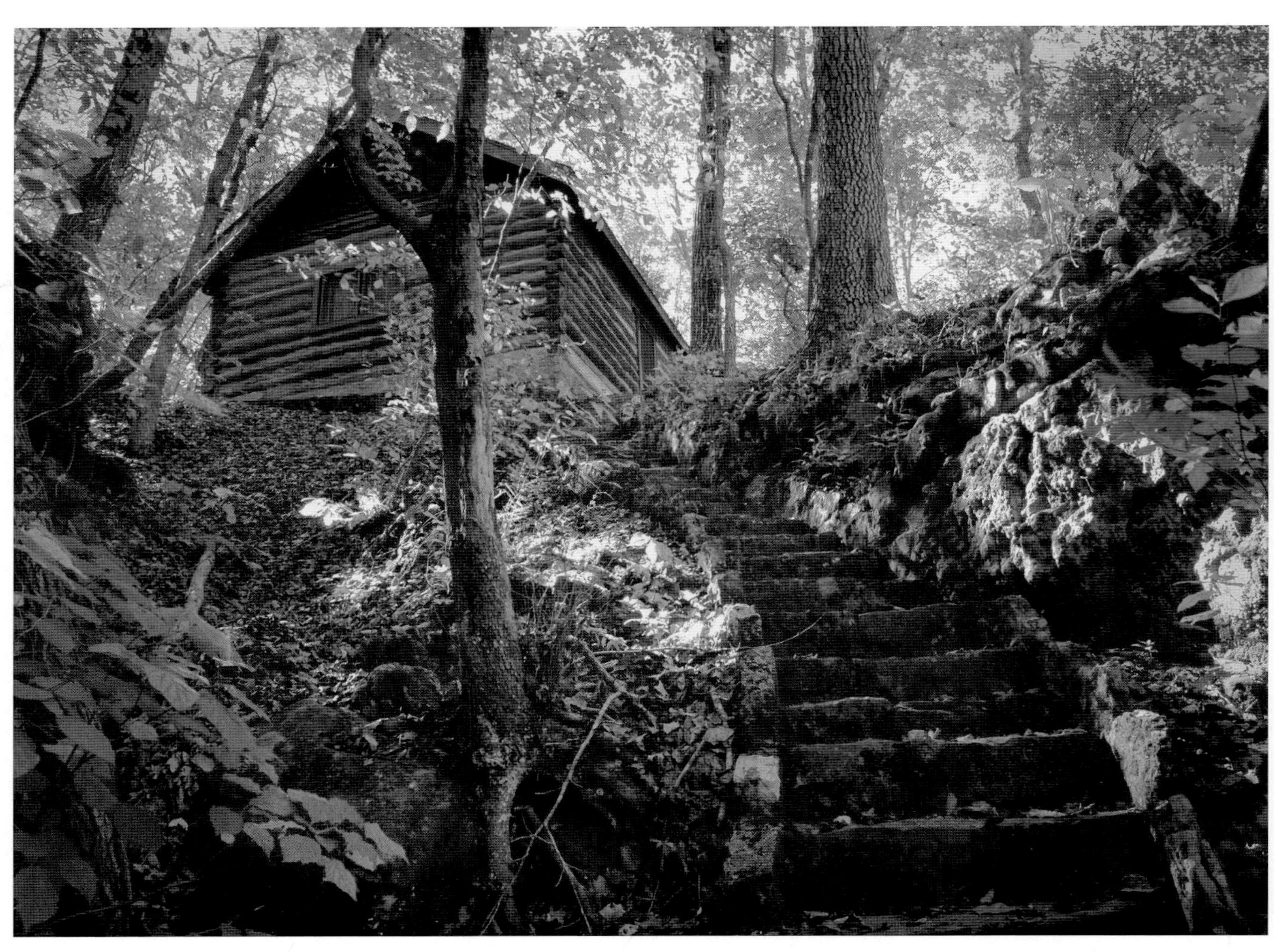

Leopold's Cabin-Caney Mountain Wildlife Refuge, Ozark County, MO

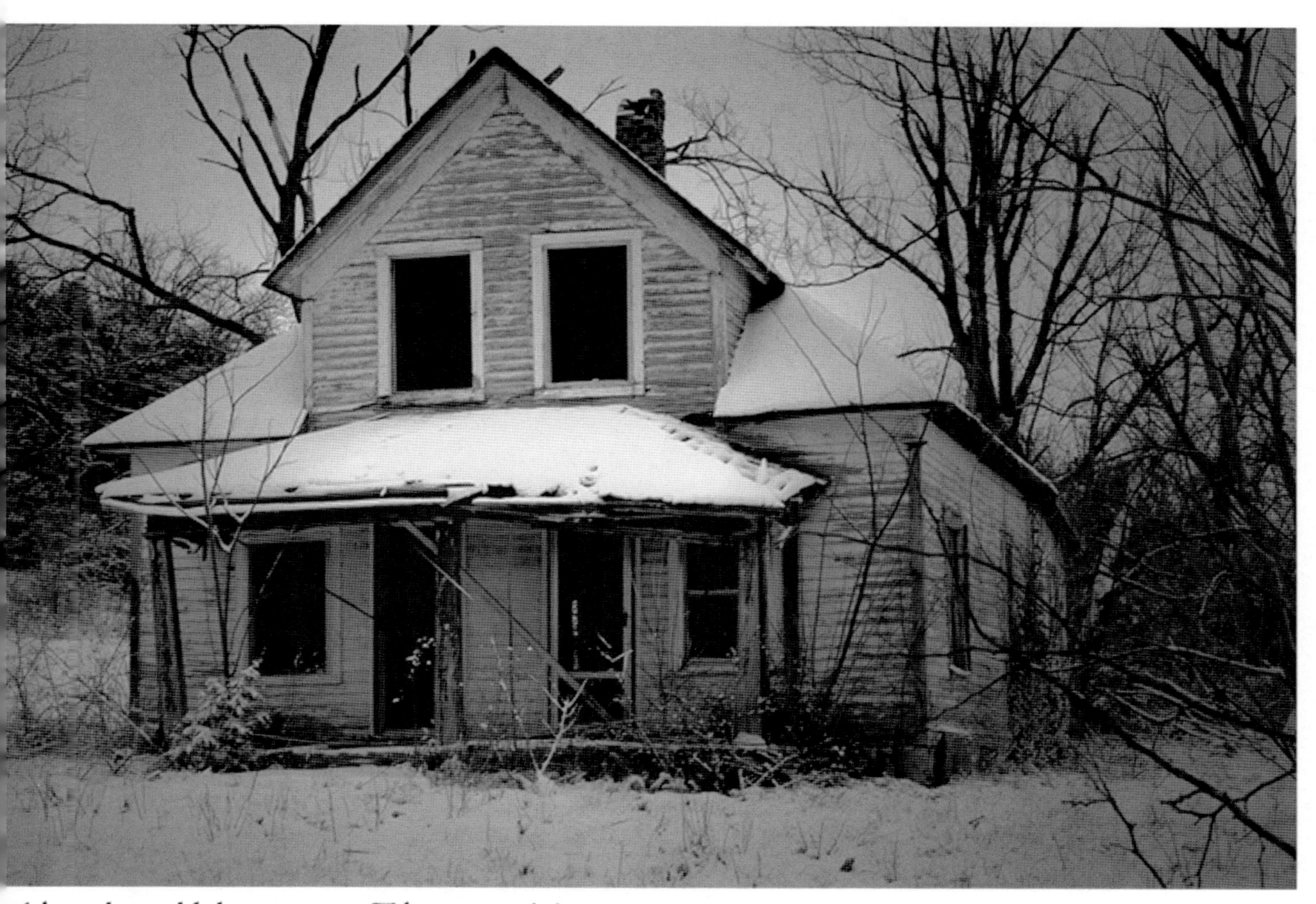

Abandoned House near Ebenezer, Missouri

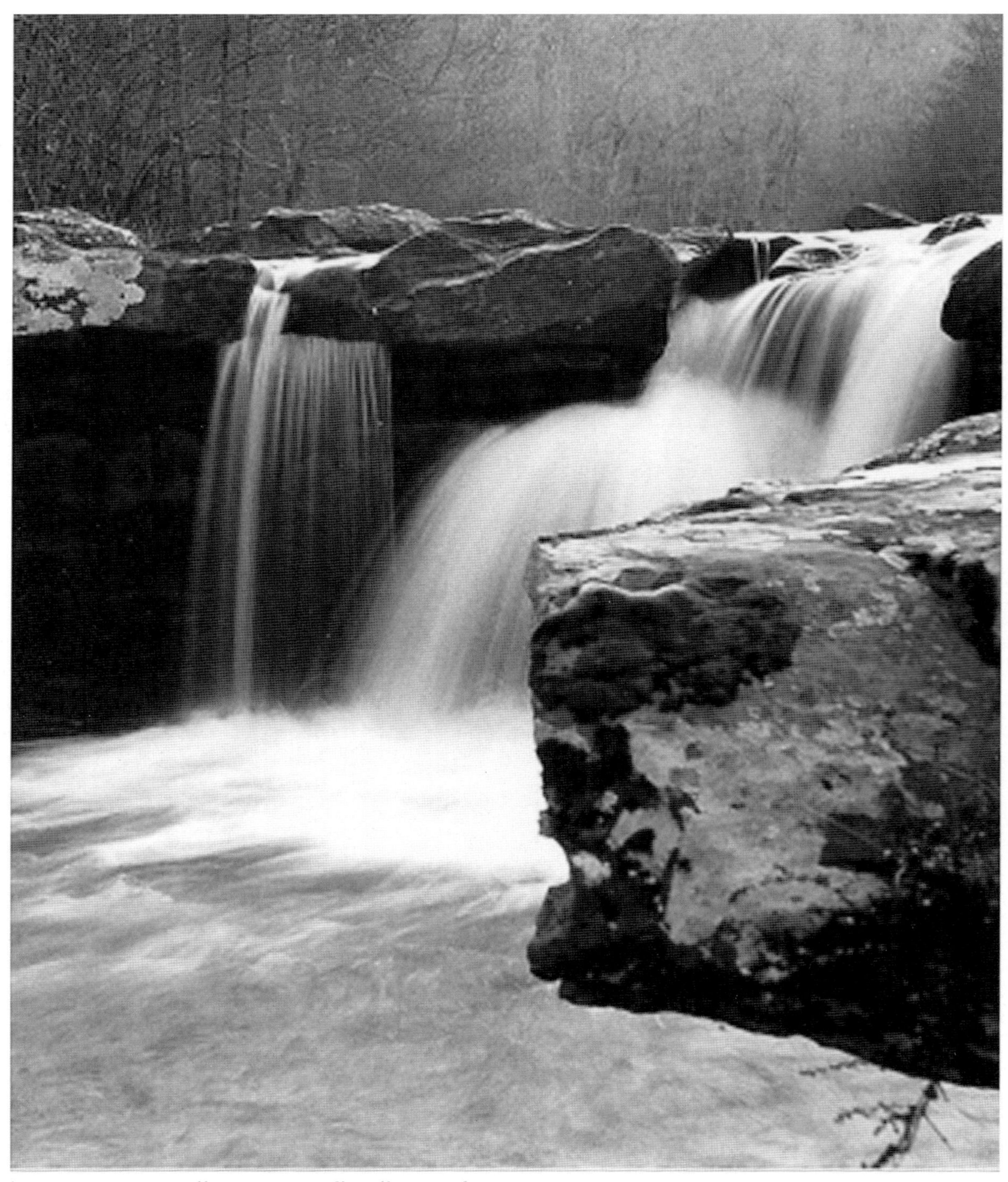

King River Falls near Fallsville, Arkansas

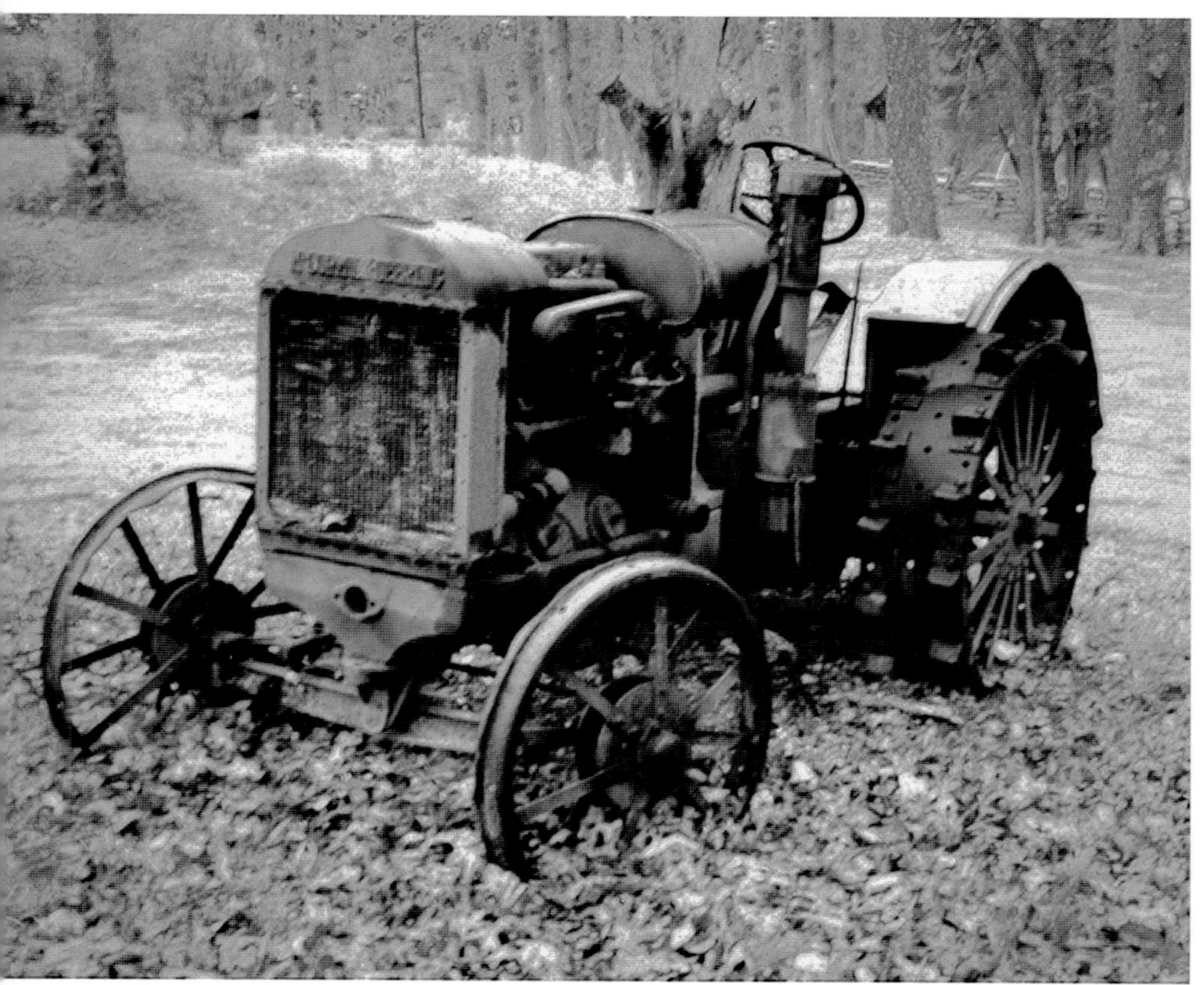

1930 McCormick Deering Tractor Model 1020 found with a tree growing through it in Mark Twain National Forest and retrieved in 1985. It resides at the forest headquarters in Ava, Missouri

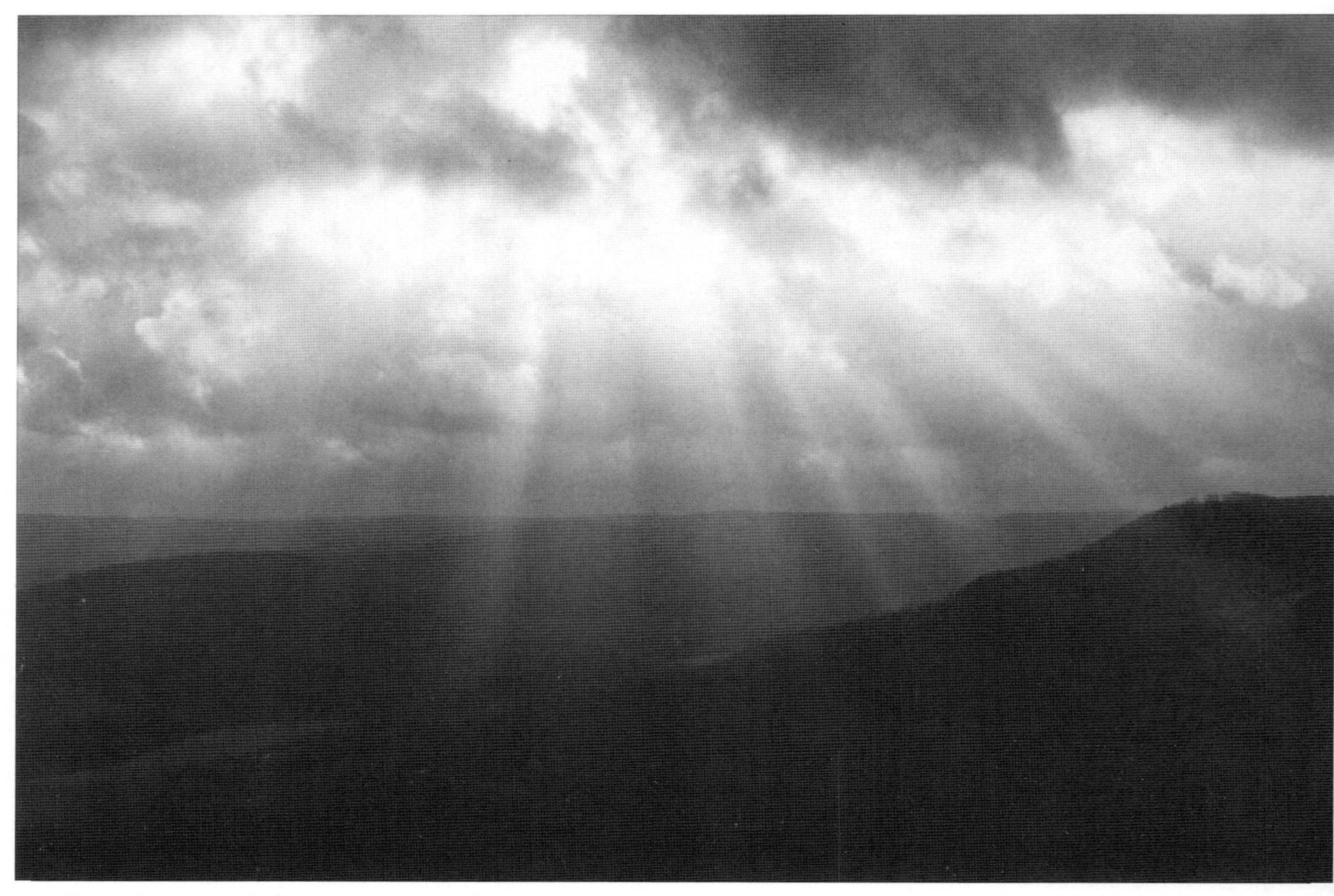

God Beams-Hwy. #7 near Jasper, AR

"Constantly think of the Universe as one living creature, embracing one being and one soul; how all is absorbed into the one consciousness of this living creature; how it compasses all things with a single purpose, and how all things work together to cause all that comes to pass, and their wonderful web and texture." (Marcus Aurelius, 170 A.D.)